ACCESS TO INFORMATION:

A Manual for Bibliographic Instruction at Iowa State University

Cathryn M. Canelas

Jan Fryer

Rae Haws

Mary Ellen Hurt

Tammy J. Lusher

Loren Peterson

Tracy C. Russell

Diana D. Shonrock

Carolyn Yorgensen, Production assistant

Ramy Hosseinie, graphic artist

Bibliographic Instruction Department

IOWA STATE UNIVERSITY
OF SCIENCE AND TECHNOLOGY

Waveland Press, Inc.
Prospect Heights, Illinois

For information about this book, write or call:
  Waveland Press, Inc.
  P.O. Box 400
  Prospect Heights, Illinois 60070
  (708) 634-0081

Copyright © 1990 by Iowa State University Research Foundation, Inc.

ISBN 0-88133-565-7

All rights reserved. No part of this book may be reproduced, stored in a retrieval system, or transmitted in any form or by any means without permission in writing from the publisher.

Printed in the United States of America

7   6   5   4   3   2   1

TABLE OF CONTENTS

Chapter 1	The Library and the Educational Process	1
Chapter 2	Intellectual Access to Information	9
Chapter 3	Locations and Services	15
Chapter 4	Developing a Search Strategy	27
Chapter 5	Finding Materials in the Library	37
Chapter 6	Using Indexing Services	43
Chapter 7	Understanding Computerized Literature Searching	53
Chapter 8	Using the Library's Catalogs	59
Appendix A	Bibliographic Instruction Objectives	79
Appendix B	Bibliography	81
Appendix C	Selected Indexing Services	84
Appendix D	Selected References Sources	89
Appendix E	Self-Help Questions	93
Appendix F	Answers to Self-Help Questions	106
Glossary		110
Search Strategy Assignment		115
Index		119

CHAPTER 1

The Library and the Educational Process

"The true university of these days is a collection of books."

--Thomas Carlyle, 1841

It would be hard to imagine a university without a library. Even more difficult to imagine is a scholar without a large body of recorded knowledge to use in the development of new knowledge. As a student at Iowa State University, you will participate in scholarship by learning how to conduct research and write the results. Using the Library will be one aspect of your participation in the scholarly process. This manual and the course Library 160 will assist you in participating fully in your education.

The Iowa State University Library is an organized and usable storehouse of the recorded knowledge of centuries of learning and scholarship. Each day new ideas, developments, and discoveries are reported in the many publications received by the Library. By learning some basic procedures and steps you will be able to seek information for your needs.

Library 160 is designed to acquaint you with the materials and services available in this Library. To assist you in the learning process, we have included self-help questions at the end of the manual in Appendix E.

Using a large research library can sometimes be intimidating. After completing the course we hope that you will feel more confident in your ability to use the Library. Remember, this Library exists to serve you. Learn how to use it and don't be afraid to ask questions.

Information, Knowledge, Scholarship

"Where is the wisdom we have lost in knowledge? Where is the knowledge we have lost in information?"

--T.S. Eliot, 1934

Webster's *New World Dictionary* defines scholarship as "the quality of knowledge a student shows; the systematized knowledge of a scholar." The three terms **information, knowledge,** and **scholarship** are intertwined and it is natural to associate one with the other. Scholarship is built from information and knowledge. The access to information and knowledge is essential for intellectual liberation and creativity.

Information sources include libraries, people, stores and offices, personal beliefs, and feelings. Don't limit yourself to one source when filling your information needs;

realize that the world is rich with information waiting for your wise and judicious use. As you gain more experience in research, you will discover more ways to make the research process meaningful and successful for you. Later chapters of this manual provide you with strategies to help you cope with and use to your best advantage all the information available. Information in its various packages is structured in different ways, so one key to the successful use of this information is to understand the organization of specific information sources. Libraries follow systematic rules of organization. The systems the Iowa State University Library use are explained briefly in this manual.

Organization of Knowledge: Cataloging and Classifying

As rational beings, humans have the need to make order from chaos. Survival in its most basic sense requires organizing skills and the ability to classify. Organization provides a rhythm to life, giving control over the many factors pulling for our attention. Classification puts like groups together, and allows for easier retrieval of the desired information. Think how chaotic a library would be if it were structured as a warehouse of books and journals lacking documentation of what was owned; lacking access to the information by author, title, or subject; and arranged not by subject discipline, but in the order purchased, or by the color of binding, or by size. Locating information under these conditions would be cumbersome and time-consuming. This is why libraries do two fundamental processes to materials as they are acquired: cataloging and classifying.

Cataloging is the written description of a publication owned by a library. Cataloging determines ownership, provides location information, and is contributed to catalogs. Catalogs can take many different forms. In a library the common forms of catalogs are a cabinet of drawers and cards called a **card catalog**, and a computer database called an **online public access catalog**. The Iowa State University Library uses three different types of catalogs: a computer catalog, SCHOLAR2, the Card Catalog, and the *ISU Serials Catalog*. Each catalog contains different ownership information for various types of publications. A description of each of these catalogs and how to use them is provided in later chapters.

In using a library, you have probably noticed that once you locate the book you want, the books around it cover the same subject. This is because librarians take great care to categorize titles by subject and use a classification system to assist in putting like things together on the shelf. The Library uses the Library of Congress Classification System, which is a detailed system of letters and numbers. The letter or letters stand for a broad subject area and the numbers signify a narrower aspect of that subject. Classification, however, is just one part of the publication's location in the Library. Each publication title is also assigned a unique notation that signifies the publication's location. This unique notation is a **call number**. The call number is your access point for finding books, periodicals, or media in the Library. Call numbers are found by using the Library's catalogs and are placed on the spine of the volume, the box in which microfilm is held, or some other noticeable place on the item for easy identification. It is important to know how to read call numbers in order to locate the publications you may need. Understanding call number order is explained in a later chapter.

The Careful Use of Knowledge

Conservation and Preservation

As a consumer and future producer of research, you have a significant role in the preservation of knowledge. The collections of the Iowa State University Library are for you and future generations. To ensure that our collections will remain for the generations intended, your cooperation in respecting the following rules is appreciated:

* **No food or drink** in the Library. Food attracts paper-eating insects, and spills from drinks cause permanent stains as well as encouraging the growth of mildew.

* **Do not eat or drink** while reading Library materials. Again, food and drink can damage the paper on which the book or periodical is printed.

* **Handle books with clean hands.** Fingerprints are often indelible.

* **A nondamaging way to remove a book from the shelf is to push back slightly the volumes on either side and grasp the desired book at mid-spine.** Or place your index finger firmly on the top of the book and tip the book towards you. Yanking at the top of the binding eventually ruins the spine covering.

* **Do not turn down the corners of pages to mark your place.** The creases will be permanent and, if the paper is brittle, the corner will break away with one fold. Laying a book face down to mark your place weakens the binding and can soil pages. The best way to mark your place is with a slip of paper.

* **Take care not to wrinkle or crumple pages when photocopying books.** If a book is bound so that it resists being pressed flat, don't force it--settle for a less than perfect image of the page you are copying. Also, glass plates on photocopy machines have been shattered from too much pressure applied when a bound volume resists being pressed flat. It is important to be careful for your own, as well as the book's, safety.

* **Damaged materials should be taken to the Circulation Department** so they can be forwarded to the Conservation Office for treatment. Minor repair problems can become major ones if they are neglected too long.

Do not attempt any repair yourself. The repair of library materials requires skill and training. Well-intentioned but ill-advised repairs often do more harm than good.

* **Take notes on a separate sheet of paper.** What you underline or write in a book may not be what the next user views as significant.

* **Keep books away from rain, bath water, hungry animals, small children, or heat sources.**

* **Handle microforms by the edges**, as you would a photograph. Remember, damage that is invisible or insignificant to the naked eye may become a major problem when the text is enlarged for reading. Smudges and scratches obliterate images, destroying information.

The collections of the Iowa State University Library are yours. Your tuition helps pay for the materials and the staff who select, care for, and help you use them. Treat library materials as you would your own possessions--with care and consideration.

Academic Integrity

The university is a community of scholars where the creation and communication of ideas has a high value. Inherent in this value is the respect for proper documentation, representation, and expression of the intellectual content of an idea. In your own work you will use information that someone else has collected or produced. This is true of **secondary research**, where you consult and use periodical articles or books. It is also true of **primary research**, where you interview, survey, or conduct controlled laboratory experiments because background research from the literature of that field should be consulted. As a researcher, you are expected to know the rights and obligations of using background information. If you are unclear about what constitutes unethical academic behavior, refer to the *Iowa State University Information Handbook* or ask a faculty member for guidance. Two areas of concern in using information are **plagiarism** and **copyright.**

Plagiarism is a significant ethical issue. The word comes from the Latin *plagiarius* meaning "one who abducts the child or slave of another, a kidnapper." (*Oxford English Dictionary*) This type of theft extended its meaning to literary theft, which is how we presently use the word. Plagiarism is the work of one person being used by another in a way that does not give credit or clearly reveal the original source. When you conduct research, keep accurate notes on the information sources you consult. Properly cite these information sources in your bibliography or list of references as part of your paper.

There are several style manuals to help you properly document of sources. Some style manuals are more suited for certain subject disciplines than others, and your instructor will usually state the style manual preferred. An annotated list of the most commonly used style manuals is provided in Appendix B.

Copyright laws exist in order to protect those who have created works and to ensure that they have control over the use of their works for a specified time. The purpose of copyright law is to guarantee the authors or creators a fair return on their investment in time, effort, and expense. The rights of the public to use information are protected by allowing reasonable nonprofit use, without payments to creators under the federal copyright law, Education and Fair Use. Most likely, the use you make of information gathered for your research project will not violate copyright law. Staff members in many areas of the Library are trained to help ensure that copyright laws are not violated. This is for the protection of library patrons as well as for the Library itself. If you have questions regarding copyright, ask a librarian for clarification.

The Self-Directed Learner

Reading, reflecting, and learning are not activities that will end once you leave the university. Libraries exist so people may be informed citizens. Learn to be comfortable in the use of libraries now and you will have a skill that shall benefit you throughout life.

CHAPTER 2

Intellectual Access to Information

We live in an information saturated society. We are bombarded with information but not all the information we receive is essential to our everyday survival nor is it needed immediately. Learning to sort valuable information from that which is not needed is an important research skill. This chapter introduces you in a very broad and general manner to the history of information and its structure.

History

Information gathering and sharing has been a basic human endeavor from the time the cave dwellers painted their first cave picture through today's modern computer systems. Structured methods of access to information, however, are a fairly recent development.

Concentrated efforts to organize information began in the nineteenth century. With the invention of the mechanical press in 1811, the publication of newspapers and journals became more efficient and profitable. As the quantity of printed material grew, the lack of a way to gain access to these publications became evident. To address this problem **periodical indexes** were developed. The first index was alphabetically arranged and was organized using broad subjects. Its main purpose was to organize the published material, on a variety of subjects, in several periodicals.

Another development during this first stage of the organization of information was the creation of **classification systems**. The Library of Congress Classification System, the Dewey Decimal System, and others allowed librarians to group books on like subjects together in a collection. Books on similar subjects were given similar call numbers, which identified the publications and gave them a place on a shelf.

After World War II, a major technological development in the organizing of information was the advent of the computer. The Lockheed Company was among the first to use a computer for storing and retrieving of information. Their computer programmers translated information from paper format to electronic format. Information stored in such an electronic format is referred to as a **database**.

This early work has been refined and has acted as the catalyst for other developments in information processing and retrieval. One of the more recent information storage inventions is the Compact Disk--Read Only Memory, or CD-ROM. Here at the Iowa State University Library the new CD-ROM workstations in the Reference Area employ this technology.

Most early databases were similar to paper indexes, providing only a referral to a published article. Today some **full text databases** are being developed to provide the full text of an article to the researcher.

Once you identify an item with the help of an index, you need to consult a library catalog to determine whether or not the Library has the needed item in its collection. Library catalogs provide an inventory of the publications in a particular library. If the item is available in a particular collection, the catalog will give the call number used in locating the item in that library. Library catalogs throughout the years have been produced in different formats. The first catalogs libraries used were in book format. Most book catalogs have been replaced by card catalogs, which were easier to update by filing cards in order. In many libraries today, the card catalog has been replaced by an online computer catalog. These catalogs provide easier and more detailed access for users. Catalogs, no matter what format, allow patrons to efficiently locate library materials by searching for publications by author, title, or subject rather than by browsing through the collection.

Structure of Information

Information comes from many sources, but it can be divided into three categories. To help visualize this concept, think of a three level-pyramid. The top level is "tertiary sources," the middle level "secondary sources," and the bottom level "primary sources."

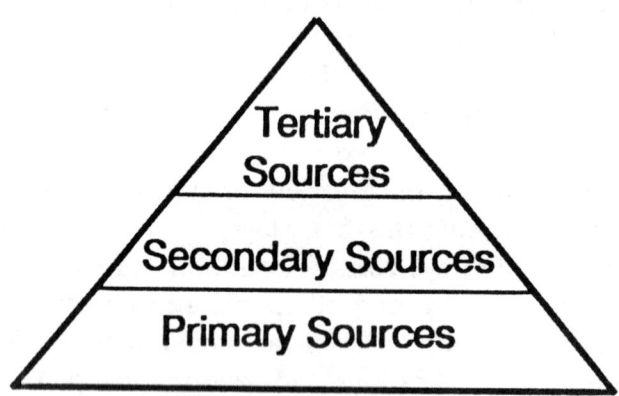

Primary sources are pieces of information generated by an individual involved in an event. Examples of primary sources are letters of correspondence, diaries, interviews, and original musical compositions. Use of primary sources can add strength to a research paper or offer an inside glance to a particular event.

Secondary sources interpret and analyze primary sources. They are once removed from the actual event described. A book about effects of the Civil War is a secondary source because the author was not actually a participant in the war. She/he is writing from a distance. A journal article that interprets the importance of an individual's contribution in a field is a secondary source. Textbooks and manuals used in courses are secondary sources of information because they interpret and analyze information contained in primary sources.

Tertiary sources of information are access points that lead you to a primary or secondary source. They reveal what is available to you. Handbooks and guides introduce you to the sources available to you in a particular subject area. An index lists recently published material. There are two types of indexes: general and subject-specific. A general index attempts to cover publications in all areas of study. A subject-specific index concentrates on the publications in one area, such as art or education. Bibliographies are lists that tell what journal articles and books have been published in an even narrower subject area or about an individual.

A **catalog** is also a tertiary source of information, but unlike the other tertiary sources that show what is available on a global level, a catalog's focus is the local level. A catalog describes and lists the material in a specific collection. By starting on the global level with an index or bibliography you can locate citations to many sources of information on a topic. To see if they are available in Parks Library you must use the catalogs that describe and list items in this particular collection.

Reference Sources

There are sources of information that can help you while you are searching for information at all levels of the information pyramid. At each of the levels you can use these sources to help clarify or verify a fact or piece of information. The first two sources can be used to clarify word selection. **Dictionaries** define, give proper pronunciation, tell the history, and indicate the usage of words. You can also check your spelling with the help of a dictionary. Dictionaries can be general in nature, like the *Webster's New Collegiate Dictionary*, or subject specific, like the *Dictionary of Military Terms*.

Thesaurus has two definitions. The **traditional thesaurus** is a list of synonyms or antonyms for words. For example, *Roget's Thesaurus* lists alternative words you can use for the same concept. Another type of thesaurus is a **controlled vocabulary thesaurus** used to search a specific database or periodical index. It is a standardized list of terms under which information in a periodical index, catalog, or database, can be found. The purpose of a controlled vocabulary thesaurus is to ensure that most of the information on a particular topic will be found by looking under particular words or word phrases. Controlled vocabulary lists for periodical indexes and databases are often published in a separate volume called the thesaurus. The *Library of Congress Subject Headings* is an example of a controlled vocabulary thesaurus. You should use the subject headings in this list to effectively gain access to the material in this Library.

Other reference sources you can use in your research are encyclopedias, biographical sources, directories, almanacs, and yearbooks. **Encyclopedias** briefly describe events, occurrences, and people. Encyclopedias can be general, such as the *World Book Encyclopedia*, or subject specific, like *McGraw-Hill Encyclopedia of Science and Technology*. **Almanacs** and **yearbooks** can give quick, precise information on a wide variety of topics. A biographical source can give you information on a person's background. *Current Biography*, and *Who's Who* are examples of biographical sources. A **directory** can lead you to organizations and individuals that might have information on your topic because it lists the names, addresses, and telephone numbers of contact people and organizations. The *Official Congressional Directory* is an example.

The history of access to information has reflected the growth and complexity of the information itself. In this chapter you have begun to learn the concepts and vocabulary related to information and its structure. If you have a basic understanding of the structure of information and its varying functions, your attempts to find the right piece of information will be more successful.

CHAPTER 3

Locations and Services

The main library building at Iowa State University is called the William Robert Parks and Ellen Sorge Parks Library. It is named after a former Iowa State University president and his wife, both of whom continue to use and support the Library. The original part of the building was completed in 1925. Additions were built in 1961, 1969, and 1983. The most recent addition is on the south and includes the glass-enclosed atrium area, which surrounds part of the original 1925 building.

First Floor

Inside the entrance on the first floor is the electronic security system, which monitors materials as they leave the Library. An alarm sound and the gate locks if you attempt to take material out of the building that has not been properly checked out. Directly in front of you as you enter the Library is the **Information Desk (1)***. Ask here if you have questions about or need directions to appropriate Library departments or special services. The **Direction Kiosk (2)**, behind this desk, also helps you to find locations in the Library.

Directly west of the entrance is the **Circulation Desk (3)** where books are checked out and where the Circulation Print-out, a list of the materials already checked out or in a special location, is kept. Your ISU ID is your library card. It permits you to borrow books for two weeks with an additional one week grace period in which to return the book before a fine begins. It is important to pay the fine at the time you return an overdue book because the fine doubles when overdue items are simply put in the book return.

To the west of Circulation is **Photoduplication (4)**. You may go to this room to have copies or transparencies made for you. Coin-operated copying machines for you to use are located on all the floors as well as in the Reference, Reserve, and Periodical Rooms. In the Photoduplication Office, you may also sign out an auditron which allows you to make multiple copies and pay for them at one time.

In the center of the first floor lobby is the **Card Catalog (5)** and terminals for the online catalog, **SCHOLAR2 (6)**. You can find more detailed information about these catalogs in later chapters of this manual.

The **Reference Desk (7)** and the **Reference Collection (8)** are located north of the Card Catalog. Librarians at this desk will answer questions and help you use the resources of the Library. The Reference collection includes handbooks, yearbooks, biographical materials, encyclopedias, and many kinds of indexes. Since these materials are in great demand, they do not circulate. Also available in this area are the sources that guide you to publications of federal and state governments as well as various international governmental organizations. Many government publications have been cataloged and are located in the General Collection. You can locate them by using SCHOLAR2 or the Card Catalog. The Reference Desk staff will help you locate those government publications not cataloged. Most of these publications can be checked out.

---

*These numbers correspond to the area numbers in the accompanying floor plans. Restrooms are indicated on the floor plans with **M** or **W**. Elevators are indicated with **E**.

In your research you will sometimes discover items you want that are not available at this Library. The **Interlibrary Loan Office (9)** provides access to materials not owned by the Iowa State University Library. Through online computer systems and other methods many types of publications including books, periodical articles, technical reports, and government documents may be obtained from other libraries, companies, individuals, and organizations. Although many materials can be obtained free of charge, there may be a fee for some items. Usually there is a waiting period of two to three weeks before this material arrives for you to use.

Today many materials--including magazines, newspapers, government publications, and books--are published in reduced size on photographic film rather than traditional paper formats. These microform publications are housed in the **Microforms Center (10)** and include: microfilm, microfiche, and microprint. You may read all three types here and you may have paper copies made from microfilm and microfiche. Also, you may borrow many items on microfiche, along with a portable reader, for use at home. Staff members are always available to help you use the equipment there.

The **Bibliographic Office (11)** is where you should come for information concerning this course.

As you go east from the Reference Room you pass by two doors on your left. These doors lead to the central stairway, which provides access to all the tiers and floors. Continuing east you pass through the **Grant Wood Foyer (12)**. The mural here and the ones in the stairway leading to the upper lobby were painted in the 1930s by a team of WPA artists under the direction of Grant Wood. The two sets are titled, "When tillage begins, other arts follow." Beyond this foyer and to the north, you will find the **Reserve Desk (13)**. Required reading is placed on reserve by faculty members to insure its availability to large numbers of students on a limited loan basis. To find the material you need, check the large notebooks on the tables. These notebooks are arranged alphabetically by department and numerically by course number. To use these materials, fill out a call slip and present it with your ID to an assistant at the desk. For your convenience, there are several photocopy machines in this room, and just south of this room is a reading area, the **Reserve Reading Room (14)**.

The glass atrium area on the first floor is just west of this reading room. Opening into the atrium are the **Seminar Room (15)** and the **New Book Room (16)**. You may be asked to come to the Seminar Room with one of your other classes for instruction in the use of library materials relevant to a particular field of study. In the New Book Reading Room you will find books newly acquired, but not necessarily newly published. These books are arranged by call number and are available for inspection for seven days. If you wish to check one out, complete the yellow postcard available in the room; you will be notified when it is available.

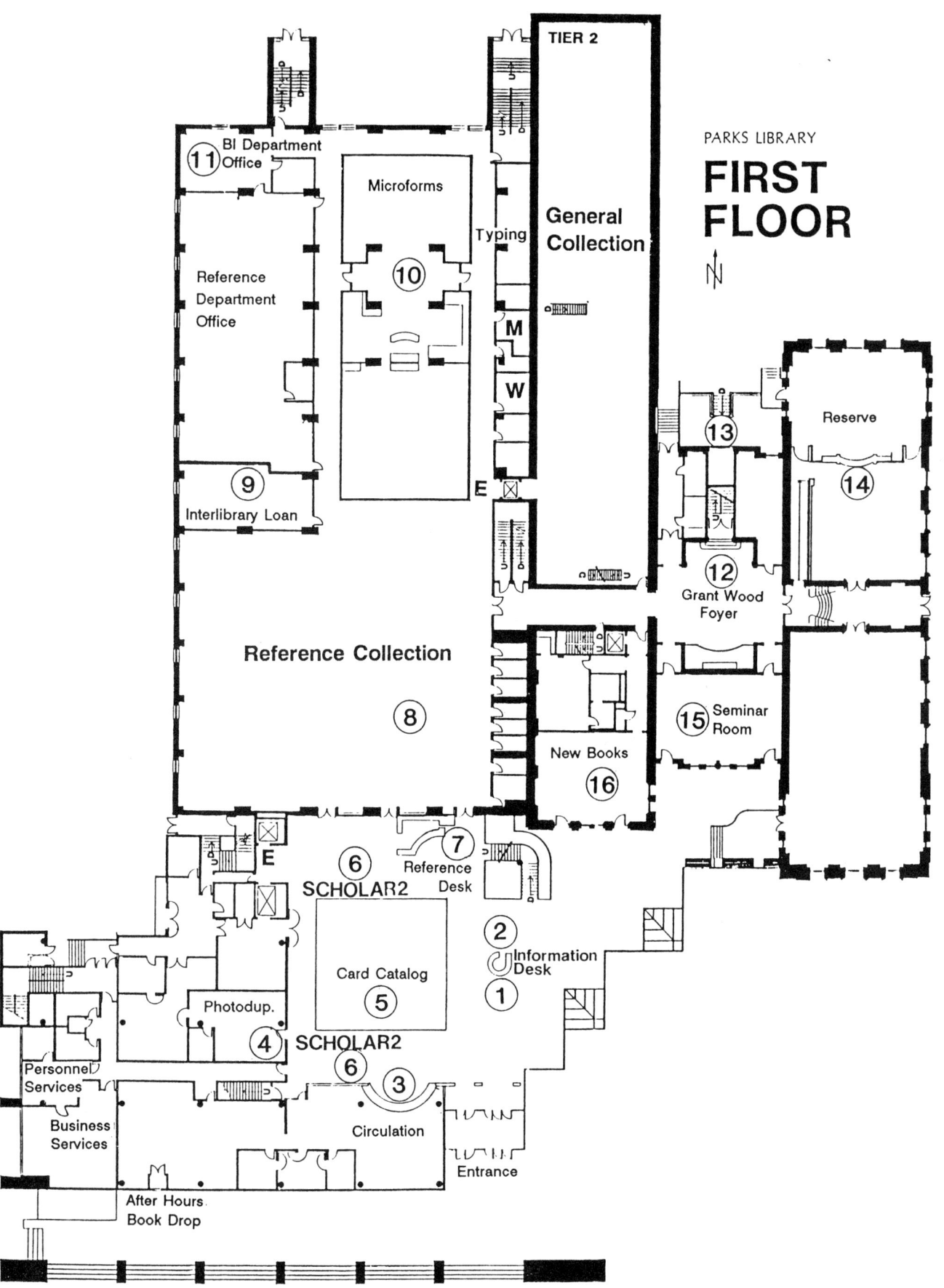

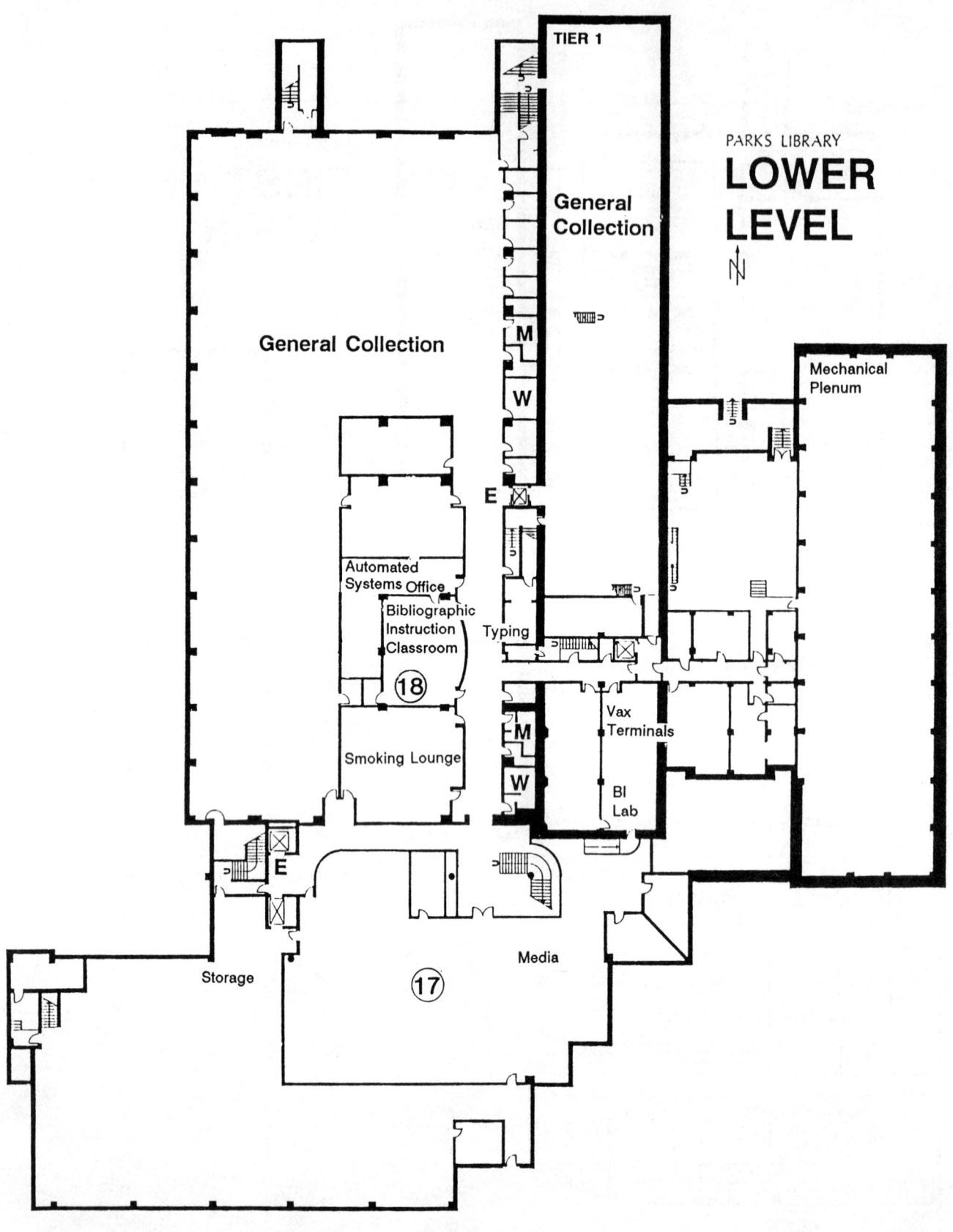

Lower Level

The **Media Center (17)** is located on the lower level of the Library's new addition. This department houses the Library's collection of videotapes, audiotapes, slides, filmstrips, and other instructional and recreational nonprint media. The Media Center's card catalog will assist you in finding the type of material you need. Reserve lists provide access to the media material placed on reserve by instructors for class use. To use media materials, you must have a current ID. The staff is always available to help you find materials and use the various media equipment. Media equipment and materials cannot be taken out of the Library. The Media Center also has a portable audio cassette tape player, an audio tape, and booklet you can check out to take an audio tape tour of this building. The tour tape is currently available in English, Mandarin Chinese, and Arabic.

The **Bibliographic Instruction Classroom (18)**, Room 32 is also located on the lower level as is the **Laboratory**, Room 84. The latter contains a number of computer terminals used to access the online catalog, SCHOLAR2, and indexes in CD-ROM format. This is used for both library staff training and student instruction.

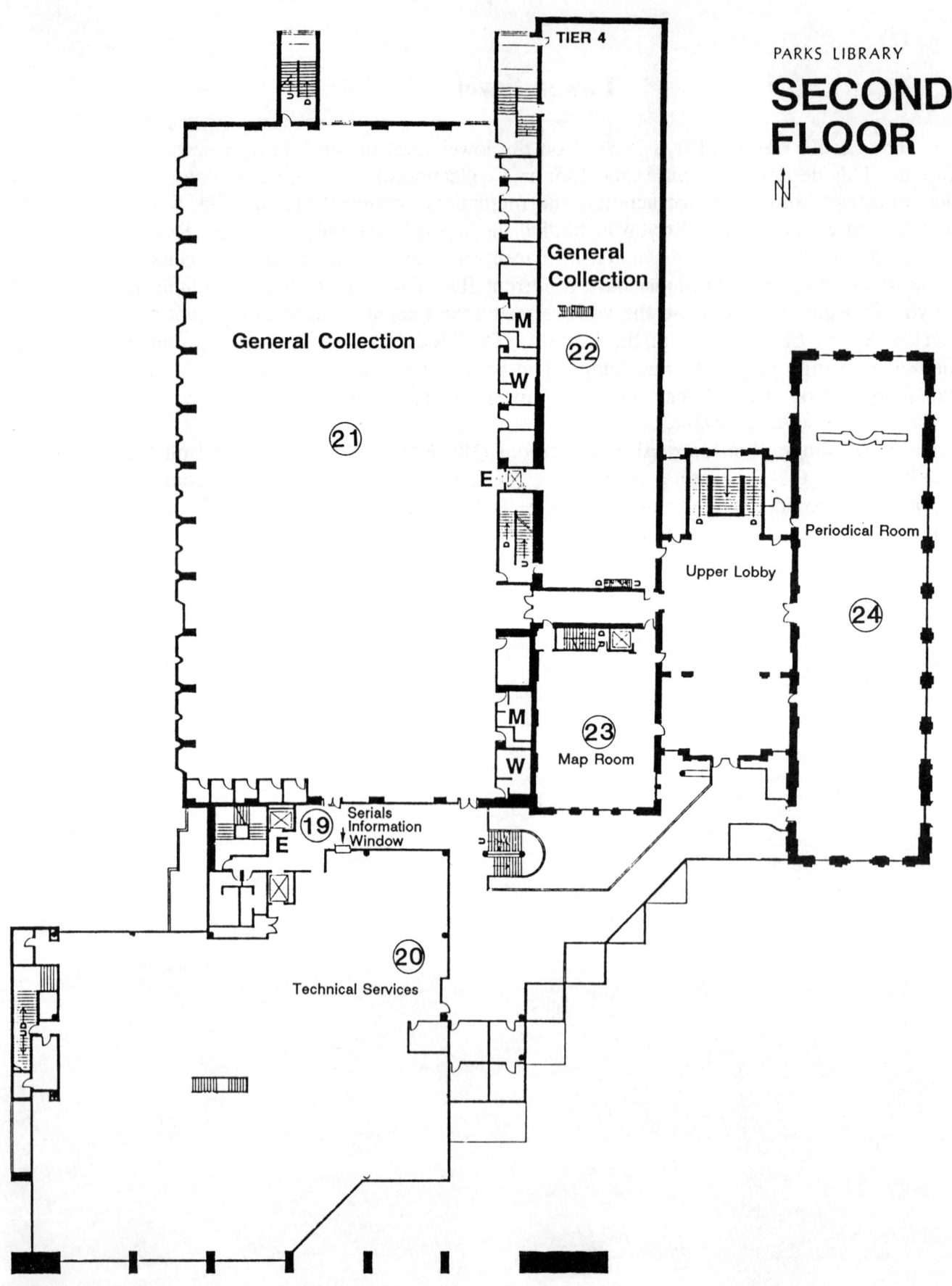

Second Floor

If you take the spiral staircase to the second floor, straight ahead and on your left is the **Serials Information Window (19)**. A staff member will assist you here if you need information about the availability of a particular issue of a periodical or magazine. The **Technical Services Area (20)** is where most of the materials for the collections are selected, ordered, processed, and cataloged.

The **General Collection (21)** and **(22)** includes the books and periodicals shelved on all floors, except the first, and on the seven tiers. The book shelves on the tiers and floors are often referred to as the **stacks**. There are signs at the ends of each row of shelving indicating what call numbers are shelved in each stack range. Study tables and carrels are located throughout the floors and tiers for your convenience. When using these areas, do not leave your personal items unattended because theft is an unfortunate but real problem. Keep your purse, briefcase, backpack, books, and calculators with you or within sight at all times.

The **Map Room (23)** is located adjacent to the upper lobby. In this room you will find topographic and geological maps as well as aerial photographs. A sizable collection of atlases and city and state maps is also found here.

The **Periodical Room (24)** is located along the east end of the second floor. Here you will find the current, unbound, issues of about 3,000 periodicals. Not all of the Library's current periodicals are shelved here. The Library has nearly 21,000 periodical titles in its collection, and most of these, including the current issues, are shelved in the General Collection on the floors and tiers. The periodicals in the Periodical Room are arranged in call number order. Some of the most heavily used periodicals are kept at the desk, and may be obtained upon presenting your ID. Also located in this room is the Library's collection of local, state, national, international, and financial newspapers. None of these publications can be checked out, but there are copy machines in the room for your use.

Third Floor

On the third floor, in addition to the shelving area of the General Collection, you will find a large study area, the **Administrative Offices (25)** of the Library, faculty and graduate study rooms, and **Group Study Rooms (26)**. These group study rooms are available to students on a first-come, first-served basis. Proper identification must be presented at the Circulation Desk in order to get a key to one of these rooms.

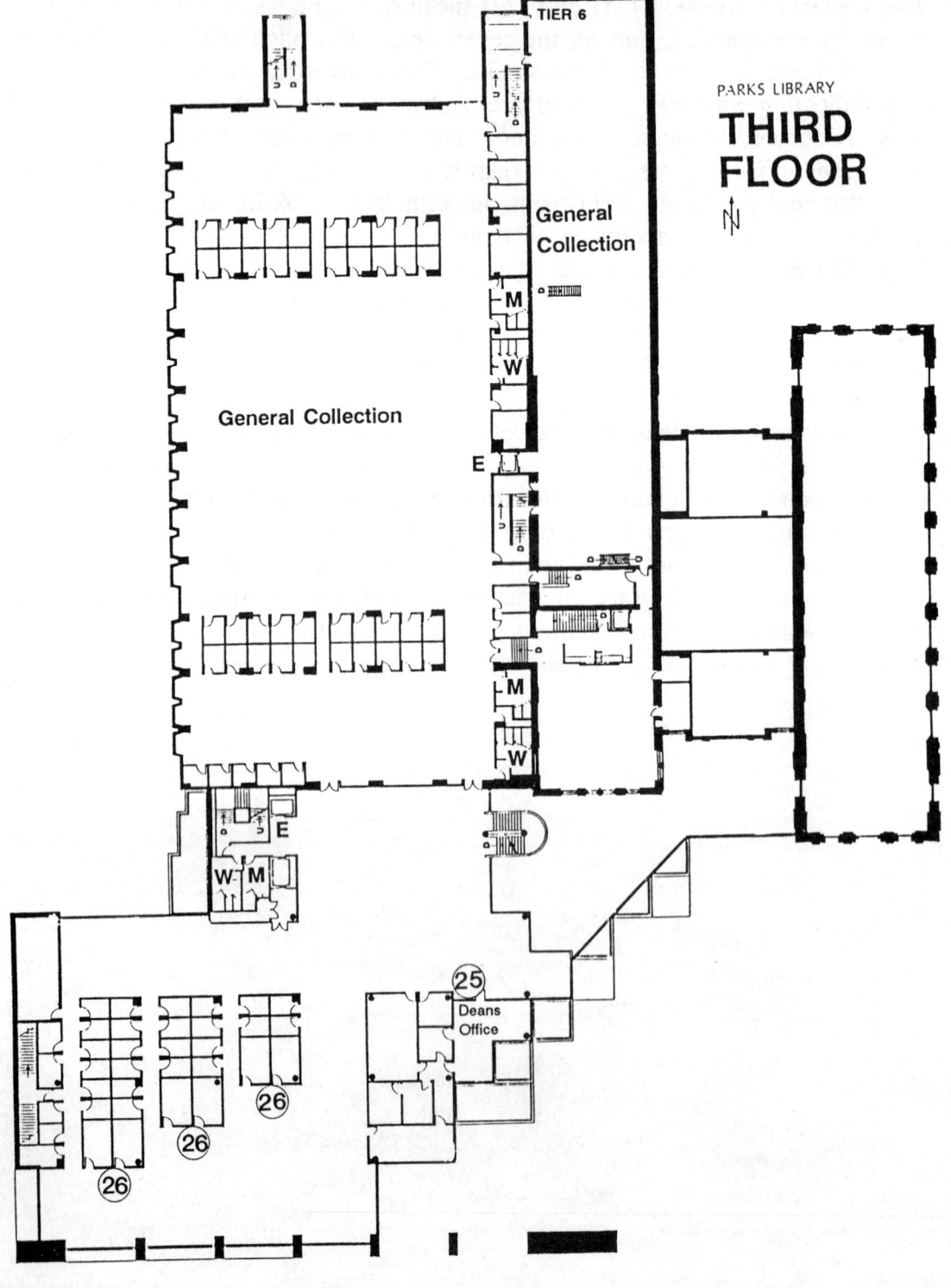

Fourth Floor

Here you will find additional shelving for the General Collection and more study space. **Special Collections (27)**, including the University Archives, is also located on this floor. Administrative records of the university, papers of faculty and staff members, as well as other historical information about ISU, are kept here. More than 5,000 rare books are also included in this collection. You may use these materials only in this area. Staff members will gladly assist you.

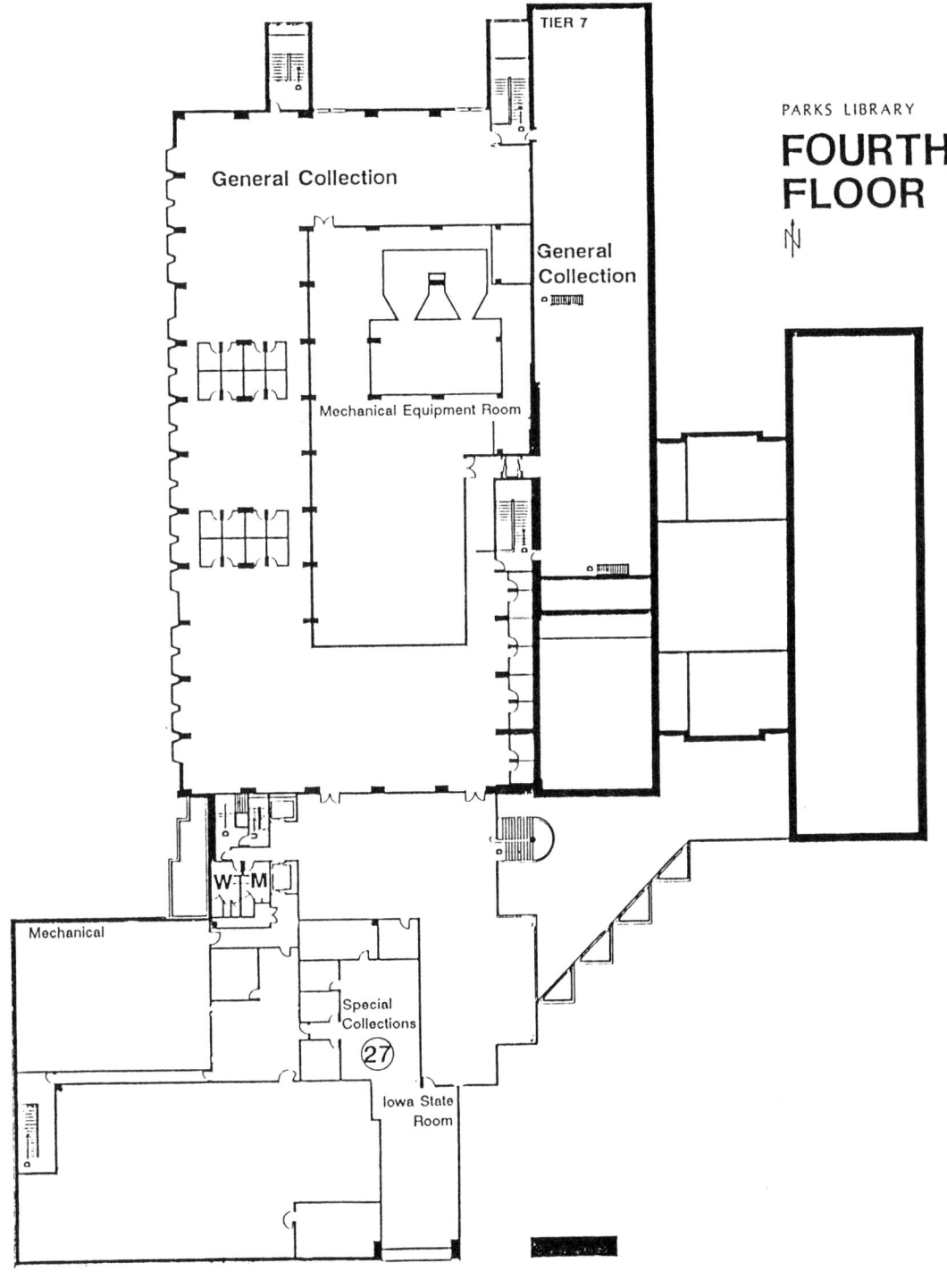

CHAPTER 4

Developing a Search Strategy

Many of your college courses will require that you gather information on a topic, analyze that information, and present your conclusions in a paper, presentation, essay test, or some other format. A **search strategy** helps you to locate information for any kind of project requiring in-depth research. A search strategy is defined in *Elsevier's Dictionary of Library Science Information and Documentation* as an "organized method of searching for information in a system." As you begin your search for information for college research or for any project, a search strategy will help you to approach the literature on any subject in an organized manner. Outlining a search strategy before you begin gathering information can save you time and wasted effort and ensure that you are able to find information appropriate for your needs. This chapter introduces the factors involved in setting up a search strategy for any topic.

Choosing a Topic

The process of selecting a topic for a research paper is closely linked to the process of finding information on that topic. Many students do not devote sufficient time or thought to topic selection and therefore have a difficult time finding information and writing their papers. Keep in mind that you may need to alter your topic according to the amount of information you find. The resources you read while researching your topic also may provide a new approach to the subject and you may decide to focus on a particular aspect, broaden it, or change it in some other way. You may want to ask your professor for help in selecting an appropriate topic before you begin looking for information. Remember, in order for your research to be successful it will require your active involvement at every stage.

When selecting a topic, your first consideration should be whether or not it is relevant to your class assignment. You will also find that researching and writing your paper is easier when the subject is of interest to you.

If the topic is one that you know almost nothing about, you need some background information in order to focus your thoughts and clarify the thesis of the paper. For instance, if you are interested in "Latin music" you might start by going to an encyclopedia and reading the entries on "Latin American music and dance," "salsa" (or any other type of Latin music), and articles about the country where that music originated. Keep in mind that general encyclopedias such as the *Academic American Encyclopedia, Encyclopedia Britannica*, or *World Book Encyclopedia* are not the only possibilities. There are also many specialized encyclopedias such as the *International Encyclopedia of Psychiatry, Psychology, Psycho-Analysis and Neurology; Encyclopedia of the American Judicial System;* or, for our sample topic, the *New Grove Dictionary of Music and Musicians*. Background information helps you clarify what you want to write about.

Brainstorming

The second step is a brainstorming process in which you explore ways that you might approach the subject you have selected. In this step you should be as creative as possible. It may help you to jot down all the ideas you can think of on a sheet of paper (see sample list, page 30). At this point you should be open and creative. Don't be afraid to list things that might not work because they may lead to other ideas and you can eliminate the unacceptable ones later. After you have listed all possible ways to approach the topic, choose one approach and elaborate on it in two or three sentences. What is the purpose of the paper? Are you describing, analyzing, or comparing? Why did you select this approach?

The result of this brainstorming process should be a list of possible ways you might explore the topic and a brief description of the approach you have selected. You should write these down and then keep this paper with you to help you as you search for information.

Defining Search Terms

Now you need to **select synonyms** for the key concepts in your topic. It is important to do this because libraries and the resources contained in them may refer to the same subject with different terms. For example, the subject "Latin music" may be listed under the terms "Latin American music," "South American music," "Hispanic American folk music," "Latino songs," or "Latin American culture." In order to be comprehensive in your information search, you may have to look under several different terms.

Narrowing the Focus

Sometimes, after beginning to collect information on your topic, you may discover that it is too broad, so you will want to narrow your focus. For example, the subject "Latin music" is a broad topic. There are many sources that cover various aspects of this subject and it would be impossible to be comprehensive in examining the literature. It would also be difficult to address all the important issues involved. Therefore, if you were interested in researching this subject it would be best to concentrate on a specific aspect of it. There are many criteria that can be applied to subjects to narrow them, including time, gender, age, or geographical area. You could also approach the topic from a specific point of view or concentrate on a subtopic. For example, rather than using "Latin music" as a topic, you could focus on "salsa" or "music in Argentina," which can be further narrowed to "tango."

BRAINSTORMING PROCESS

Music of Latin America → specific country?
   Salsa – Cuba to New York — History of Salsa?
   Merengue   Development of Salsa?
   Tango – Argentina   Oscar De Leon
   Cumbia – Colombia   Celia Cruz
                                    Grupo Niche

Protest Songs? Relationships between political situations and texts of protest songs.

Music – Instruments, texts, rhythms, melody, harmony, dances. Role of music in society – entertainment, cultural expression, social commentary.

TOPIC CHOSEN FOR PAPER

My focus: The forces involved in the development of salsa from its beginning in Cuba in the 1940s to its current status. I will concentrate on social rather than musical factors, i.e., its role in retention of Latin culture in a foreign country (USA), the degree of its acceptance in mainstream musical circles, how the text reflects Latin culture.

Broadening the Context

This step, the opposite of looking at specific aspects of a topic, is to put your subject in a broader context. There are two reasons that this step is important. First of all, information on a subject may be embedded in a larger work. For example, a textbook on South American music may have a chapter discussing the music of Bolivia; however, because it is not the focus of the entire work, it would not be listed in the library's catalog under "Music of Bolivia." This step is also important in instances where you cannot locate enough information on your topic and you need to broaden your focus in order to find enough material. For example, if you are interested in writing about the musical instrument "bandoneon" (the focal instrument of the Argentine tango), you may not find many sources focusing on that topic. You will find more information if you broaden your topic to "tango" or "Argentine music."

Types of Sources

There are many sources of information, both in and outside the library. When you are researching a topic, you need to understand the kinds of information that different types of sources are likely to provide. Many students are tempted to take the easy way out and simply look up a book or two on their subject. While this may be adequate for a simple project, you can expand the variety and amount of information you find by exploring different types of sources.

While you do your research you should be aware that information is time-specific. In other words, you should know that the currency of your topic will affect when, where, and how much information you will find. For example, if you looked in a 1986 periodical index for information about the dance, "lambada," you would not find anything. Always keep in mind which time period or year information would have been produced about your topic.

This section describes how information is produced and where you can find different kinds of information. To illustrate, we will use the subject "the development of salsa."

Newspapers

Newspapers are an excellent source of current factual information. Current events and other "hot" topics will appear in print there first. For example, when salsa first became popular in the United States in the 1940s, newspapers were the first sources to cover this new dance craze.

Newspapers often reflect a local perspective that can be invaluable in research. It might be interesting to compare and contrast American and Cuban newspaper articles about salsa. Do not overlook editorials, which are often good sources of varying opinions.

Remember that access to newspapers and articles in them varies considerably. For instance, major newspaper such as the *New York Times* or *Washington Post* produce their own indexes which are updated every three to six months. Major newspapers are also indexed by such periodical indexes as the *National Newspaper Index*. However, most local newspapers, such as the Ames **Daily Tribune,** are not indexed at all. Therefore, it is very difficult to find articles in these local papers by subject.

Magazines

Magazines are geared toward broad audiences and cover a wide variety of subjects. Because of their popular nature, magazines often feature colorful photographs, enticing headlines, and advertising. Keep in mind that authors of magazine articles are usually professional writers who are not specialists in the field. The information you find may be informative and up-to-date, but it may not be as in-depth or as authoritative as that found in other sources.

When a topic becomes important and/or of interest to the general public, articles in magazines such as *Time* and *Newsweek* will appear two to three months after their appearance in newspapers.

Journals

Journals are excellent sources of in-depth information. Unlike magazines, journals are often geared toward a specific subject area and the articles are written by experts in that field. Journals are the best place to find recent research results and current trends in particular disciplines. Since they require in-depth research, journal articles begin to appear at least six months after an event or issue has become important. After salsa developed into a genre of musical importance, articles began to appear in journals. To find journal articles on this topic you could begin with the *Music Index*, where you would find citations to journals such as the *Latin American Music Review*.

Government Publications

Government publications are issued at city, state, national, and international levels. They are often excellent sources of statistical information. Since the government is the single largest funder of research, documents are produced dealing with all disciplines. There are also many publications dealing with a wide variety of government-related policies and issues.

Government publications would not be an obvious source for a paper on salsa, but, since the government generates information on all topics, some information might be found. For instance, government-funded organizations such as the Archive of Folk Song, a special collection of the Library of Congress, might publish bibliographies and other research relating to the development of salsa.

Books

Books provide many different types of information depending on their length, scope, and purpose. They are often excellent sources for a historical perspective or overview of a subject. By the time a book is published about a developing and changing topic such as salsa, it will be one or two years out of date.

Reference books such as encyclopedias, almanacs, and dictionaries can provide you with factual information. A reference book is often an excellent place to start gathering information because encyclopedia articles give you a brief overview of a subject. Some reference books also list other sources on your subject that you may want to obtain for further reading.

People

Don't forget that people can be excellent sources of information. Your professors can refer you to books, articles, or specialists in the subject area you are researching. In some cases you may want to survey people in your community regarding their opinions on an issue. A conversation with an expert or someone who is closely associated with a topic you are researching can add a unique, personal perspective seldom found in printed sources.

Other Sources

Be creative in gathering your information. You can also gather information from student organizations, professional organizations, archives, associations, chambers of commerce, and many others.

Evaluating Information

While you are gathering information for your paper there are several things you should keep in mind. You should be evaluating the information you collect at every step. Ask yourself, is it authoritative? Is it written by an expert or is it just an editor's opinion? Is this the kind of information you need? Does the author betray a bias? If so, what is the bias? When was the information produced? The date could affect the currency or credibility of what is stated. If you have been approaching your topic from a political science point of view, could your argument benefit if you read articles from a psychological, sociological, or historical point of view? You may want to include multidisciplinary points of view.

Once you have gathered most of your information and are about to begin writing, take another look at what you have compiled from your research. Ask yourself if your thesis would benefit from other types of information. For example, if you have books and journal articles, would your argument be strengthened by adding some statistics? Or if you have a lot of statistics, could you use an expert's opinion? Do you have enough information? Are there any holes in your argument? Once you have answered these questions, you are ready to begin writing your paper.

Sample Checklist

A research strategy can help you organize your thoughts and make your time spent doing research more efficient. Remember to follow these steps:

- [ ] Select a topic.
- [ ] Brainstorm and gather background information.
- [ ] Narrow or broaden your topic as needed.
- [ ] Gather information from a variety of sources and points of view.
- [ ] Evaluate the information you have collected and look for holes in your argument.

Using the techniques outlined above you will find writing papers more productive and less frustrating.

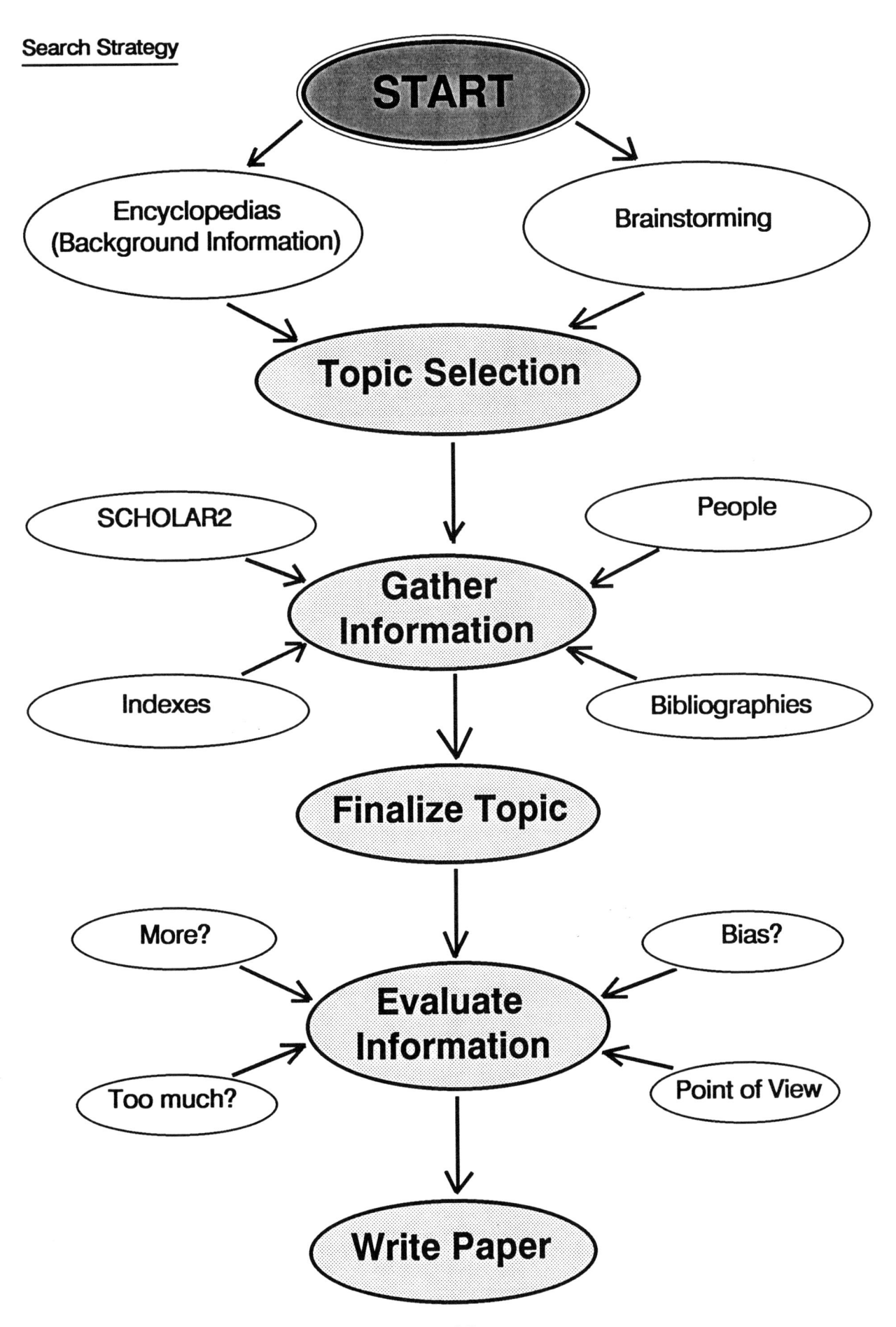

Search Strategy

- **START**
  - Encyclopedias (Background Information)
  - Brainstorming
- **Topic Selection**
- **Gather Information**
  - SCHOLAR2
  - People
  - Indexes
  - Bibliographies
- **Finalize Topic**
- **Evaluate Information**
  - More?
  - Bias?
  - Too much?
  - Point of View
- **Write Paper**

CHAPTER 5

Finding Materials in the Library

One of the ways that libraries arrange publications is to use a system of classification. The system this Library uses is called the Library of Congress Classification System. This system was first developed by the Library of Congress in Washington, D.C., which originally served as the library to the Congress of the United States, and now serves the nation's libraries in a variety of broad functions.

The Library of Congress Classification System uses both letters and numbers to identify the subject of a book:

Library of Congress Classification System

Class Letters
R--Medicine
S--Agriculture
T--Technology

Subdivision under class letter T--Technology
TA--Civil Engineering
TC--Hydraulic Engineering
TD--Environmental Technology

Subdivision under TD--Environmental Technology
TD159--Municipal engineering
TD172--Environmental pollution
TD196--Environmental pollutants

Subdivision under TD196--Environmental Pollutants
TD196 .A25--Acid rain
TD196 .A34--Agricultural chemicals
TD196 .D48--Detergents

One way you might use to search for material on a subject is to just browse through the stacks. If you browse for books and serials on a topic, you can use this first pair of letters and numbers. For instance, since you know that **TD 196** is the subject classification for environmental pollutants, you can go straight to that call number area rather than looking in a catalog. The various catalogs specify the location of each item, but most of the Library's collection is located in the General Collection on the floors and tiers. The **Locations of Call Numbers** guide tells you where call numbers are located in the collection. Keep in mind that, depending on your subject, browsing may not be the most effective way to search for materials since there may be hundreds of sources in a particular area.

LOCATIONS OF CALL NUMBERS
in the Parks Library's
GENeral Collection

Call Numbers	Location
A-AZ	Lower Level
B-BD, BH-BJ	Lower Level
BF	Floor 3
BL-BX	Lower Level
C-CT	Floor 2
D-DX	Floor 2
E, F	Floor 2
G-GV	Floor 2
H-HX	Floor 3
ISU	Tier 1
J-JX	Tier 2
K-KZ	Tier 2
L-LT	Floor 3
M-MT	Lower Level
N-NX	Lower Level
P-PZ	Floor 4
Q	Tier 4
QA-QD	Floor 2
QE	Tier 4
QH	Tier 3
QK	Lower Level
QL	Tier 3
QM-QR	Tier 5
R-RZ	Tier 5
S-SB	Tier 1
SD-SK	Lower Level
SOUN (Media)	Lower Level
T-TJ	Tier 6
TK-TP	Tier 7
TR	Lower Level
TS	Tier 7
TT-TX	Lower Level
U-UH	Tier 4
V-VM	Tier 4
VIDEO (Media)	Lower Level
Z	Tier 3

When you come to the Library to look for a specific book on your topic, you need to have what is called the **complete call number**. Additional letters and numbers are added to a subject classification to form a **call number,** which is a unique identification for a title. Call number is an old-fashioned term from the days when the public was not allowed to go into the "stacks" and only a member of the library staff could go to where the books were shelved to retrieve the item requested or "called for" by the user. The complete call number for a book by Marshall E. Wilcher, *The Politics of Acid Rain*, is formed in this way:

TD196--The Library of Congress Classification for Environmental pollutants

A25--Subclass for acid rain

W54--Unique identifying letters and numbers for this book

1989-- Date of publication

This call number may also be written horizontally on one line as:

TD196 .A25 .W54 1989

A call number is made up of at least two letter/number parts; it can have more than two parts but not fewer. Once you have the complete call number for a book or periodical to locate it on the shelf, first determine from the catalog where it is located in the Library's collection. If it is in the General Collection, use the first letter or letters of the call number and the Locations of Call Numbers guide to tell you on which floor or tier to look. In this case, the **TD** publications are found on Tier 6. The locator maps on each floor will tell you where to find each major letter group. The signs on the end of each row of book stacks indicate which call numbers are shelved in each row; these are called **stack range indicators**, and look like this:

TD172 .E54 -
TD201 .A3

Since all the books are arranged alphabetically by call number, you'll see that the books marked **T**, a single letter, come before the ones marked **TA** and the books marked **TA** come before the ones marked **TD**.

Next look for the number **196** in the **TD** section as a whole number.

TD34 will come before **TD196**

Now look for the second letter **A** within the **TD196** section.

TD196   will come before   **TD196**
A   **B**

The next part is sometimes confusing. The numbers that follow the second letter are read as decimals; that is, **25** is **.25**. So within the **TD196** section, one marked:

TD196   will come before   **TD196**
A25   **A7**

This order is correct! Although the number **25** may look larger than **7**, the decimal **.25** is smaller than **.7**, which is the same as **.70**.

In the next part of the call number, **W54**, 54 is also treated as a decimal .54.

The final part of this call number is the date, **1989.** This is the year of publication, but not all call numbers include this date. Those with dates are shelved in chronological order with the earliest date shelved first.

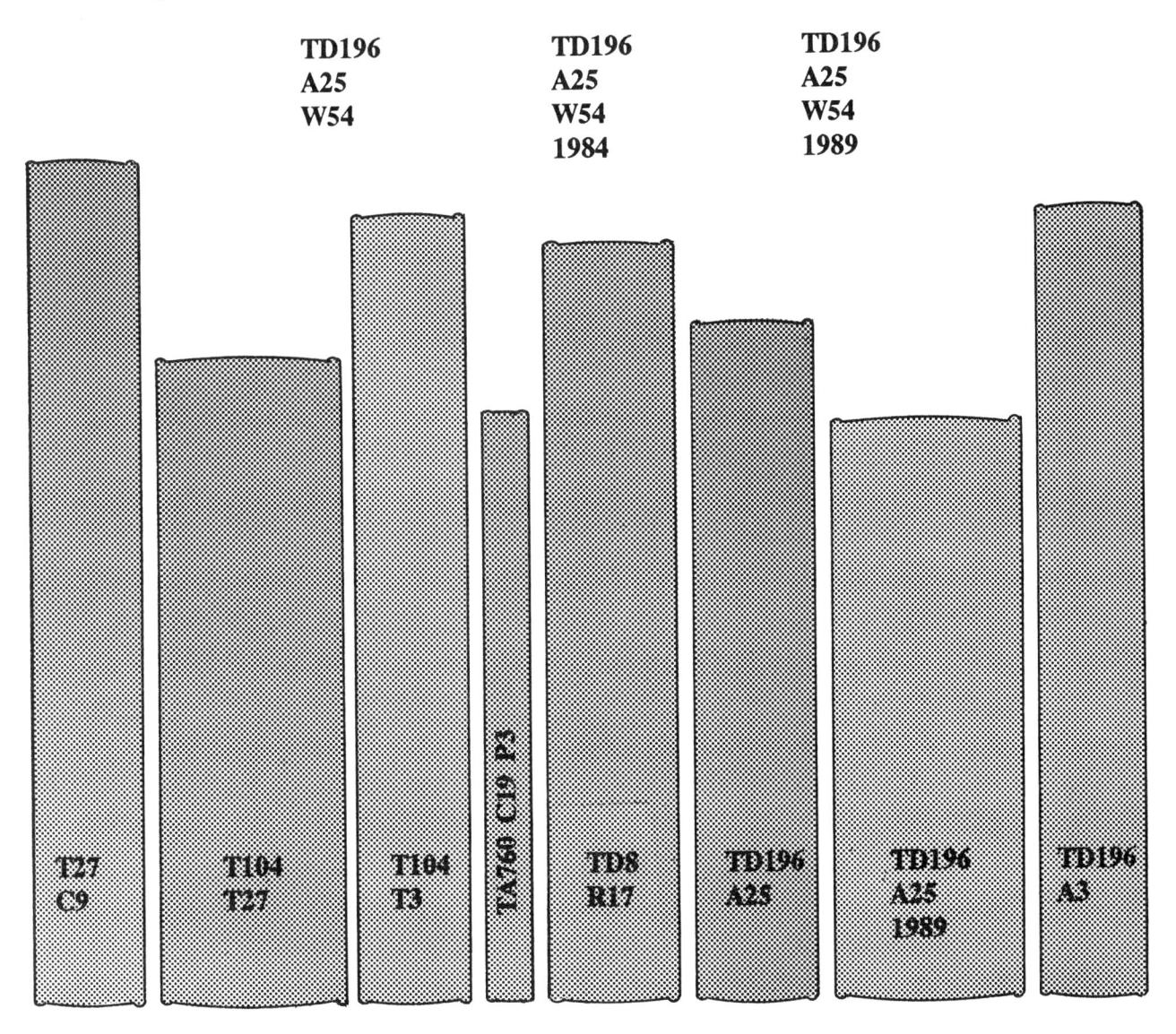

	TD196	**TD196**	**TD196**
	A25	**A25**	**A25**
	W54	**W54**	**W54**
		1984	**1989**

Books on shelf (left to right):
- T27 C9
- T104 T27
- T104 T3
- TA760 C19 P3
- TD8 R17
- TD196 A25
- TD196 A25 1989
- TD196 A3

Figure 5.1 Sample shelving arrangement using the Library of Congress Classification System.

41

CHAPTER 6

Using Indexing Services

In Chapter 5 you learned about the classification system used in the ISU Library and you learned how to locate specific call numbers on the floors and tiers. In this chapter you will learn about **indexing services** which are used to identify articles within periodicals and newspapers as well as from books, government publications, pamphlets, and other publications on specific topics.

Periodical Literature

While books are lengthy narratives usually devoted to a single subject, periodical literature is quite different. Issues of periodicals usually contain a number of articles on various topics written by different authors. **Periodicals** are published on a continuing basis--daily, weekly, monthly, quarterly, or at some other regular interval. Periodicals are also called **magazines, journals,** and **serials.** Magazines usually contain articles of general interest while the articles in journals report the results of research and/or are of a more scholarly nature. The word **serial** is an umbrella term for magazines, journals, newspapers, periodicals, proceedings, and papers.

Periodicals are valuable resources because they contain the most recent information available on a topic. Periodicals often include articles on current events or research long before a book may be written on the topic. They may also contain book reviews, news items, and other timely material.

The problem with using periodical literature is that it is so vast; it would be impossible to find an article on a specific topic or a review of a particular motion picture or book by simply leafing through issues of periodicals. Therefore, **indexing services,** which list individual articles by subject and author, have been developed. This chapter, will help you learn to use a variety of indexing services.

Locating Periodical Articles

The most efficient way to locate a periodical article on a specific topic is to use an **indexing service**; periodical articles are **not** listed in SCHOLAR2, the card catalog, or the *ISU Serials Catalog*. Indexing services provide subject access to periodical literature as well as to books and other publications by listing **citations** to individual items. Citations contain the pertinent information necessary to identify a publication and may include the author, title of the article or book, title of the periodical, volume number, issue number, page(s), column (in a newspaper), date, publisher, place of publication, language, and the existence of such features as a bibliography, photographs, portraits, or diagrams. Not every element is included in every citation; however, care should be taken to write down all of the information given in a citation to ensure that you will be able to locate the article later. This information is also necessary for the preparation of footnotes and bibliographies in research papers and projects.

Below are four samples of **citations** found in indexing services. It is important to understand the unique features of citations so you can decide whether your citation is to a book, a chapter of a book, a periodical article, or a newspaper article. Once you have decided on your citation type then you are able to check the appropriate catalogs to see if the item is owned by the Library.

1. Citations to **books** include the author's name, the title of the book, the publisher's name, the place of publication, the date of publication, and number of pages. Sometimes the price is included.

673
Kern, M. Thirty-second politics: political advertising in the eighties. New York: Praeger, 1989, 237 pp. $45.00/$16.95

2. Citations to **chapters in books** are more difficult to identify, especially if the chapters have been written by various authors. The citation includes the author and title of the chapter, then the editor's name is listed, and the title of the book, the publisher's name, the place of publication, the date of publication, and the page numbers. If the book is part of a series there may also be a volume listed.

692
Costley, C. L. and Brucks, M. The roles of product knowledge and age on children's responses to deceptive advertising. Bloom, P. N., ed. Advances in marketing and public policy, Vol. 1. Greenwich, CT: JAI Press, 1987, pp. 41-63.

3. Citations to **periodical articles** usually include the title of the article, author of the article, the title of the periodical, the volume number, issue number, the page numbers where the article is located, and the date of issue of the periodical.

907
Searleman, A. and Carter, H. The effectiveness of different types of pragmatic implications found in commercials to mislead subjects. Applied Cognitive Psychology 2(4):265-272, Oct.-Dec. 1988.

4. Citations to **newspaper articles** usually include the title of the newspaper article, the author's name, the length of the article, the title of the newspaper, the newspaper's issue date, the page number where the article can be found, the section of the newspaper, and the column on the page.

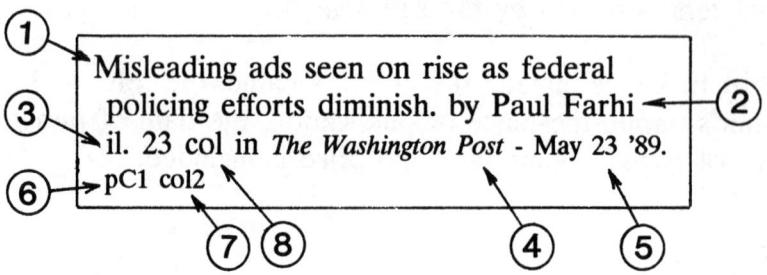

```
①↘
   Misleading ads seen on rise as federal
③↘  policing efforts diminish. by Paul Farhi ←②
   ↘il. 23 col in The Washington Post - May 23 '89.
⑥→ →pC1 col2
      ⑦⑧              ④      ⑤
```

1. Title

2. Author

3. Illustration

4. Title of the newspaper

5. Date

6. Section and page

7. Length of article (in inches)

8. Column Location

Some indexing services also provide short summaries of the publications being indexed; **abstracts** and **indexing services** that include them are sometimes referred to as **abstracting services.** Below is a sample of a citation to a periodical article and its corresponding abstract from *Communications Abstracts*.

Indexing services are available in **paper, microform,** and/or **electronic** formats. Selected indexing services in the Library are available in electronic format mounted on **compact disk (CD-ROM)** workstations while others can be accessed **online** to databases mounted on computers located across the country. Chapter 7 provides more information about electronic indexing services.

Selecting Appropriate Indexing Service

It is important to use the appropriate indexing service to locate information for your topic. Factors to take into consideration include your subject, your level of expertise, and the depth of coverage of a specific indexing service. If you need assistance in choosing an indexing service, ask a reference librarian or use the *Guide to Indexing Services*. Copies of this volume are located at the Reference Desk and on tables in the Reference Area.

The *Guide to Indexing Services* is a list of the indexes available in the Reference Area in Parks Library. It is designed to help you select an indexing service by either broad subject category or by the title of the indexing service. The guide is divided into two sections: subject (white pages) and title (yellow pages). Below is a sample page from the subject section.

SUBJECT HEADING	TITLE	CALL NUMBER	DATE
ADMINISTRATION	SAGE PUBLIC ADMINISTRATION, ABSTRACTS	A/I JA1 A1S23	1974-
ADMINISTRATION	SOCIAL SCIENCES AND HUMANITIES INDEX	AI13 IN7	1907-1974
ADMINISTRATION	SOCIAL SCIENCES INDEX	TABLE 1	1974-
ADMINISTRATION	**UNITED STATES POLITICAL SCIENCE DOCUMENTS	A/I JA1 A11U5	1975-
ADMINISTRATION- -USE ALSO 'MANAGEMENT SCIENCE','INDUSTRIAL ADMINISTRATION'			
ADMINISTRATION-MUNICIPAL	URBAN AFFAIRS ABSTRACTS	TABLE 5	1979-
ADVERTISING	BIBLIOGRAPHIC ANNUAL IN SPEECH COMMUNICATION	PN4121 A11B52	1970-75
ADVERTISING	BUSINESS INDEX	TABLE 3	LAST 5 YR
ADVERTISING	BUSINESS PERIODICALS INDEX	TABLE 3	1958-
ADVERTISING	COMMUNICATION ABSTRACTS	TABLE 5	1978-
ADVERTISING	TOPICATOR	A/I HF5801 A11T6	1965-
ADVERTISING- -USE ALSO 'BUSINESS AND FINANCE'			
AEROSPACE ENGINEERING	AGARD INDEX OF PUBLICATIONS	TL500 N63A25	1952-73
AEROSPACE ENGINEERING	APPLIED SCIENCE AND TECHNOLOGY INDEX	TABLE 9	1913-
AEROSPACE ENGINEERING	**EI ENGINEERING CONFERENCE INDEX	A/I TA5 E36X	1985-
AEROSPACE ENGINEERING	**ENGINEERING INDEX	TABLE 9	1884-

Notice that the subject headings in the left-hand column in the sample page are quite broad, so you may need to use your imagination. For example, if your topic is **television advertising** you will not find that subject in the left-hand column, but you will find the subject **advertising.** It is important for you to note that there are five different indexing services available in the Library that provide citations to materials on advertising. In addition, note the suggestion to also try the broader term **business and finance** in this same guide. Usually you will **not** find the subject of your paper in this guide, but rather the broad area of study under which your topic would fall. If you have questions as to the appropriate term(s) to look under or how to select an indexing service, you can also ask a reference librarian.

Titles of indexing services are listed in the next column. The symbols to the left of the title indicate if this indexing service can also be searched online using **SEARCHLINE** or **LARS.** Call numbers and/or locations for the indexing services in

the Reference Area are found in the third column. All of the indexing services listed in this guide are available in the Reference Area in one of four locations:
1. The tall shelves on the west side of the room
2. The shorter shelves, called **A/I shelves**, on the east side of the room
3. The numbered tables on the east side of the room
4. The CD-ROM area at the south end of the room.

A floor plan showing the arrangement of the Reference Area can be found in the front of the *Guide to Indexing Services*. The chart below can also be used to interpret the location information given in the third column.

Area Designation   **Location in Reference Room**

Call number (L11 E463)   Tall shelves, west
A/I call number (A/I QH540 E27)   Shorter shelves, east
Numbered table (Table 6)   Tables, east

The last column on the right side of the page shows the dates of the Library's holdings of a particular indexing service. The hyphen (--) after the date indicates that the Library still receives the indexing service.

If you know the title of an indexing service, you can use the title section (yellow pages) of the *Guide to Indexing Services* to determine its location in the Reference Area as well as the dates of the Library's holdings. Look at the following sample:

TITLE	CALL NUMBER	DATE
BUSINESS INDEX	TABLE 3	LAST 5 YRS
BUSINESS PERIODICALS INDEX	TABLE 3	1958-
CADMIUM ABSTRACTS	QD181 C3C3	GEN: 1977-1979
**CAMBRIDGE SCIENTIFIC BIOCHEMISTRY ABSTRACTS,	QH601 B5611X	1973-
**CAMBRIDGE SCIENTIFIC BIOCHEMISTRY ABSTRACTS,	QP551 A1N8211X	1971-
CANADIAN GOVERNMENT PUBLICATIONS	Z1373 C16C	1953-78
CARCINOGENESIS ABSTRACTS	RC261 A1C17	1963-
CATALOG OF SELECTED DOCUMENTS IN PSYCHOLOGY	BF1 C33	1971-
CATALOGUE OF PUBLIC DOCOMENTS OF THE CONGRESS	Z1223 A13	1895-1940
CERAMIC ABSTRACTS	TP785 AM35C	1922-

Traditional Indexing Services

Until the last fifteen years or so, the researcher had very little choice of format of indexing services; they were available in paper and microform. Now, however, indexing services can also be searched using the computer. Chapter 7 provides more information about computerized literature searching.

The arrangement of subject headings in traditional paper or microform indexing services determines how you locate the citations within it. There are two basic forms of arrangement in traditional indexing services: **alphabetical** or one-step indexes in which the subject headings are arranged alphabetically with citations listed immediately after each heading; and **numerical** or two-step indexes in which the researcher first uses an alphabetical list of subjects, the subject index, and then turns to a separate numerical list of citations to determine the full bibliographical information for an article.

Following is an example from the *Business Periodicals Index,* an **alphabetical** index. Notice that the **subject headings** are printed in boldface type on the left of the columns and arranged alphabetically. Just below the subject heading **advertising** are the words **see also** followed by related subject headings, one of which is **deceptive advertising**. These are examples of **crossreferences**. The purpose of cross references (see, see also) is to direct you to other subject headings you can look under in order to find articles on related topics as well as to help you narrow your topic. Citations to articles and other publications follow the cross references. Notice too, the **subheadings**, which are centered and in boldface type. They may also lead to articles on narrower aspects of a topic. In this example the word **credibility** is a subheading; it also has a crossreference to the word **deceptive advertising**.

Sometimes you will look up a topic in the indexing service and under the subject heading or the subheading will be the word **see** followed by one or more subject headings but no citations to articles. The crossreference **see** refers you to valid subject heading(s) you should use to find articles on your topic.

Advertising
See also
Creativity in advertising
Deceptive advertising
Direct mail advertising
Direct response advertising
Display of merchandise
Advertising: art, science, or business? L. Bogart. *J Advert Res* 28:47-52 D '88-Ja '89
PR on the offensive: we can do better than ads [marketing mix] D. Edelman. *Advert Age* 60:20 Mr 13 '89
Stoking the engine of the economy. D. F. Helm, Jr. *Mark Commun* 12:48 N '87

Credibility
See also
Deceptive advertising
Ad reporters exploit pull of the press [taking advantage of credibility of real reporter] P. Winters. *Advert Age* 59:30 Ap 4 '88

Sometimes indexing services are published in **microform format**. Microform indexes are similar to alphabetical indexes in paper in that their subject headings are arranged alphabetically followed by citations to articles and other publications. Like other alphabetical indexes, they involve a one-step look-up process. Unfortunately, microform indexes generally do not include as many cross references as paper indexing services. Often you must be creative in thinking of alternative subject headings or ask a reference librarian if you need assistance. In *Magazine Index,* an indexing service published in microform format, the term **deceptive advertising** was not used; instead, you must look under **advertising campaigns** and its subheading **ethical aspects**. Below is a sample citation from *Magazine Index*.

      ADVERTISING CAMPAIGNS
         ETHICAL ASPECTS

      Lying with a smile on Madison Avenue.
      (ads for Isuzu and other companies blatantly lie)
      il *U.S. News & World Report* v102 - Feb 23'87 - p58 (1).

      Numerical indexes, often called **abstracting services**, differ from alphabetical indexes because they involve going through two steps to locate a citation for a publication. They usually include abstracts of the publications indexed and tend to focus on a narrower range of subjects. In addition to citations to periodical articles, numerical indexes often include citations to technical reports, proceedings of meetings, books, government publications, and non-English language works.

      To use a numerical index, you must first look up your topic in the **subject index** section of the indexing service. The subject index is often found at the end of an issue or bound volume, or sometimes in a separate volume. With the subject heading you find one or more **citation numbers** and frequently these will be associated with various descriptive words or phrases. In addition, some numerical indexing services provide separate author indexes, institutional indexes, geographical indexes, technical report indexes, and so on, which provide additional access points.

      The second step in using a numerical index is to find the citation number and its corresponding citation in the main entry section of the indexing service.

      Below is a portion of a page from the subject index to *Communications Abstracts* and its corresponding citation. Notice that the subject heading is **advertising deception**.

Subject Index	Citation & Abstract
Advertising Deception, 574, 612, 620, 692, 907, 1133, 1182, 1342	**574** Kamins, M. A. and Marks, L. J. Advertising puffery: the impact of using two-sided claims on product attitude and purchase intention. Journal of Advertising 16(4):6-15, 1987. ADVERTISING DECEPTION. ADVERTISING EFFECTS. ADVERTISING STRATEGIES. CONSUMER BEHAVIOR. For this study, 172 college student subjects participated in an experiment in which half (86) were randomly assigned to one of four treatment groups. Each group was exposed to one of two types of advertising appeals (one-sided or two-sided refutational) combined with one of two levels of puffery (low versus high), and then given a disconfirming product trial. Data from the subjects was analyzed through the use of a 2 X 2 factorial analysis of variance design with appeal type and level of puffery as independent variables.

In this example, the citation number **574** in the subject index leads you to an article in a journal titled *Journal of Advertising*. Included with the citation is an **abstract** or summary of the article, a feature often found in numerical indexing services. Although this example is a citation to a periodical article, you may encounter citations to many types of publications in numerical indexing services.

When using either alphabetical or numerical indexing services it is important to take the time to examine the volume to determine how it is organized. Often, in the front of the indexing service you will find directions for its use, as well as lists of publications indexed and their abbreviations, lists of abbreviations used in the citations, and other information about the coverage and scope of the service. Depending on your topic, it may be necessary to use several indexing services to cover all aspects of a subject. In that case, you may need to consult the *Guide to Indexing Services* again to identify other appropriate indexing services to use.

Following is a list of frequently used traditional indexing services. There is a more extensive list in Appendix C that also includes brief descriptions of the indexing services.

Abbreviated Listing

Table 9	Applied Science and Technology Index
Table 6	Art Index
Table 8	Biological and Agricultural Index
Table 3	Business Index (microform)
Table 3	Business Periodicals Index
Table 5	Communications Abstracts
Table 6	Education Index
Table 6	ERIC - Current Index to Journals in Education (CIJE) Resources in Education
Table 5	General Science Index
Table 2	Humanities Index
Table 1 & 2	Magazine Index (microform)
Table 1	Newspaper Index
Table 1	Public Affairs Information Service. Bulletin (PAIS)
Table 2	Psychological Abstracts
Table 1	Readers Guide to Periodical Literature
Table 1	Social Sciences Index

CHAPTER 7

Understanding Computerized Literature Searching

Many of the indexing services discussed in Chapter 6 have been converted to electronic formats utilizing both large mainframe computers as well as microcomputers and compact disk (CD-ROM) technology. In addition, some indexing services are only available online and do not have a paper counterpart. When indexing services are in this format, they are often referred to as **databases.** Searching of these databases is referred to as **computerized literature searching**.

There are certain advantages in using the computer to search databases instead of looking through paper indexing services to locate information for your research projects. First, you save time by rapid retrieval of citations spanning several years without looking in several annual indexes. Second, complex, multiterm searches that would be difficult to execute in a paper indexing service are easily performed using Boolean logic. **Boolean logic** involves using the connectors **and, or,** and **not** to combine the concepts involved in your topic. For example, in a traditional index you can look up **deceptive advertising** or you can look up **automobile industry** but not both concepts at once. Using a computerized indexing service and Boolean operators, you can combine these terms so that the citations you retrieve will be about deceptive advertising in the automobile industry. Third, searches can be modified while the search is in progress, thus offering greater flexibility. For example, if a particular subject term does not retrieve any records for publications, you can substitute alternate terms and continue the search. Fourth, computerized literature searching frees you from the time-consuming task of hand-copying citations because search results can be printed and/or downloaded to a diskette in minutes.

It is not always appropriate to use a computerized version of an indexing service. One drawback of using the computer to search various databases is that most do not cover materials published earlier than the mid-1960s and some begin as recently as the mid-1980s; therefore, retrospective searching is often not possible in these services. You may want to consult with a reference librarian about the suitability of your topic for a computerized literature search and for assistance in choosing the appropriate database or indexing service.

There are three ways to perform computerized literature searches in Parks Library.

1. Compact disk indexing services (**CD-ROMs**) are do-it-yourself search services of selected databases mounted at workstations in the Reference Area. They are available at no cost to you.

2. **SEARCHLINE** is a do-it-yourself computerized literature service, available nights and weekends, which provides you with the opportunity to search online databases mounted on remote mainframe computers. There is a nominal charge for using SEARCHLINE and you must attend a training session to learn how to formulate and execute your searches.

3. **LARS**--Library's Automated Retrieval Service. LARS searches are performed online by a librarian who consults with you before and during

your search about appropriate search terms and other aspects of formulating your search strategy. There is a fee for LARS searches performed online, covering the database connect time, telecommunications, and printing of citations. The amount of the fee is depends on the length and complexity of the search as well as the database searched.

Regardless of which service you use, it is advisable to follow these steps to ensure a successful search:

1. **Plan your search in advance.**
   Write your search topic in one sentence.

   Example: Deceptive advertising in the automobile industry.

2. **Identify the main ideas or concepts in your topic.**
   Most search topics contain two to three concepts. These usually can be stated in one-to two-word phrases. The example above contains two concepts, **deceptive advertising** and **automobile industry**. Sometimes you will have more than two concepts, but remember to select only the most important ideas in your topic as concepts.

3. **Choose additional search terms.**
   The main concepts in your topic should provide your first group of search terms. However, the words used in indexing services may be different from those you have chosen. Examine your concepts to see if you can identify synonyms, related terms, plurals, and tenses which will also form part of your search statement.

   Example: Deceptive advertising in the automobile industry.

First Concept	Second Concept
deceptive advertising	automobile industry
deception	automobiles
advertisement	automobile dealer
false advertising	cars

Sometimes it is useful to use a **thesaurus** to help you identify alternate terms for your search. For assistance in locating the appropriate thesaurus for your topic, ask a Reference librarian. A thesaurus is a list of subject descriptors used in a database. It contains definitions, related terms and synonyms, and hierarchies of broader and narrower terms describing a given subject.

4. **Connect your search terms with the Boolean operators.**
Boolean operators are used to indicate the relationships among your search terms.

or   **Or** is used to combine synonyms or related terms. When you use **or** between search terms, you will retrieve citations that include at least one of the search terms in the citation itself or the abstract. Using **or** broadens a search.

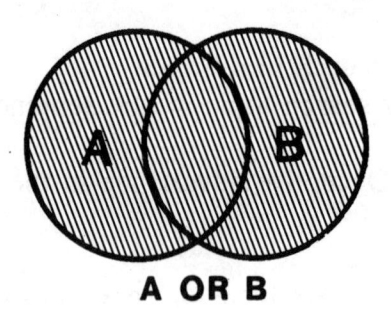

A OR B

and   **And** is used to combine search terms when all of them must be included in the citation or abstract. **And** narrows a search.

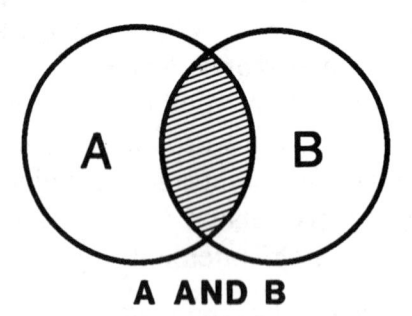

A AND B

not   **Not** is used to exclude citations to publications in which a certain term or terms occur. It should be used very carefully because relevant citations may be eliminated along with those you want to eliminate. **Not** narrows a search.

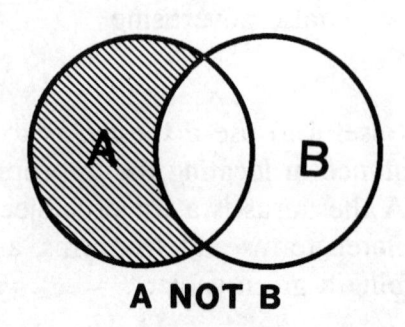

A NOT B

5. **Choose a database and service.**
    Choosing a computerized indexing service or database is similar to choosing a traditional indexing service. The most important factor to take into consideration is the subject of your search. A second factor to consider is the purpose of your research: are you giving a three minute talk or writing a twenty page research paper? A general interest database may satisfy the needs of the talk; however, you may need to use a more scholarly database for a research paper. As was mentioned earlier, a third factor to consider is the time span of the subject of your research. Some databases have only been available in electronic formats for a few years. Depending on the nature of your topic, you may need to use a combination of traditional and computerized indexing services. For example, if you are writing a paper on "Deceptive Advertising in the Automobile Industry," you may wish to use the CD-ROM service **Business Periodicals Index**. It includes citations to business related publications issued from July 1982 until the present. However, if you wish to include a historical perspective in your paper, you may wish to consult the paper version of this service, also called *Business Periodicals Index*, which includes citations to publications issued since 1958. If you need assistance in selecting a database, ask a reference librarian or consult the *Guide to Indexing Services*.

As of this writing, the following indexing services are available in Parks Library on CD-ROM:

Agricola (Includes citations to publications related to agriculture.)
Applied Science & Technology Index
Business Periodicals Index
Dissertation Abstracts
ERIC (Includes citations to publications related to education.)
MLA Bibliography (Includes citations related to language and literature.)
Marcive (Includes citations to U. S. Federal government publications.)
Readers' Guide to Periodical Literature
Social Sciences Index

Other databases are available on CD-ROM in Parks Library that are not indexing services; *Grolier Electronic Encyclopedia* is the computerized edition of *Academic American Encyclopedia*, a paper product. *County City Data Book*, a popular source for statistical information, is published in both paper and CD-ROM formats.

Additional computerized indexing services are available through the SEARCHLINE and LARS online search services. Newspapers, journals, and other full-text databases are also available online. If you have questions about these services, consult a reference librarian.

CHAPTER 8

Using the Library's Catalogs

A library catalog is a list of the books, magazines, newspapers, and other materials in its collection or, as they are often called, the library's **holdings**. At Parks Library there are three different catalogs: **SCHOLAR2**, the online catalog; the **Card Catalog**, which is divided into two parts--"Authors and Titles" and "Subjects", and the *ISU Serials Catalog*. Each of these catalogs lists part of the Library's collections. The one you use depends on what you are looking for.

SCHOLAR2, the online catalog, contains **books** cataloged since **1978** and all **serials**. The Library is currently working on a project to convert all of its old records into machine readable form, which is why many books published before 1978 can be found on SCHOLAR2. But the only way to be sure that the Library does not have a book published before 1978 is to check the Card Catalog.

The precursor of SCHOLAR2 is the Card Catalog. It contains records for books received by the Library from the time it was established to 1988. Currently only title cards are being filed. So, if you need a new book it is best to use SCHOLAR2.

The third catalog, the *ISU Serials Catalog*, lists in alphabetical order all the magazines, journals, newspapers, and other serial publications owned by the Library. Also known as the "red books," copies are located in various locations all over the Library. You will find that although magazines can be located on SCHOLAR2, searching may be easier using the *ISU Serials Catalog*.

The Online Catalog

Computers are powerful research tools. It is possible to search through hundreds of thousands of documents in seconds. SCHOLAR2 is a database of the books and magazines that the Library owns. It can be searched like the other databases that were discussed in Chapter 7. This section covers the basics of using SCHOLAR2 and provides a few hints to help you use it more efficiently.

Basic Searching

This is the welcome screen for SCHOLAR2.

WELCOME TO SCHOLAR2

THE ONLINE PUBLIC CATALOG OF THE IOWA STATE UNIVERSITY LIBRARY

The Online Catalog contains records for books cataloged since 1978 and for all cataloged serials. Individual articles in periodicals are not indexed in the Online Catalog. Pre-1978 books are continually being added to the SCHOLAR2 database.

Use Command:	When Searching for:
t	titles
a	authors
s	subject headings
k	keywords in authors, titles, subjects

Need help? Type m for more information.

TYPE a for introduction to author searches, t for title searches, s for subject searches, and k for keyword searches.
TYPE COMMAND AND PRESS RETURN==>

Basic search commands are listed here for you. Most of the time when you use SCHOLAR2 this will be the first screen you see. You do **not** have to go back to this screen to begin a search. It is possible to begin a search from **any** screen. If you wish to return to the introductory screen, type **e** for end and <Return>.

The basic search commands are:

Title--type **T**   [title of book] <Return>
Author--type **A**   [author's name, last name first] <Return>
Subject--type **S**   [Library of Congress Subject Heading] <Return>
Keyword--type **K**   [subject words] <Return>

Tips for using SCHOLAR2:

* SCHOLAR2 does not differentiate between upper and lower case.

* Punctuation and accent marks are ignored.

* When performing a title search, begin with the first significant word because SCHOLAR2 does not recognize articles such as "the" as the first word in a title. For example, type *Lion the Witch and the Wardrobe* rather than *The Lion the Witch and the Wardrobe*.

* You must know the exact title for a title search.

* In author searches the last name must be typed in first: Lewis C. S.

* You must use Library of Congress Subject Headings for subject searches.

* You must use two dashes (--) for subheadings when performing subject searches.

The Title Search

To locate a book on SCHOLAR2 type:
T Prison Crowding: A Psychological Perspective

The search will result in the following screen.

```
SCHOLAR2 SEARCH REQUEST: T=PRISON CROWDING A PSYCHOLOGICAL PERSPECTIVE
BIBLIOGRAPHIC RECORD -- NO. 1 OF 1 ENTRIES FOUND

Paulus, Paul B.   ①                              ②
        Prison crowding : a psychological perspective / Paul B. Paulus with the
collaboration of Verne C. Cox and Garvin McCain. -- New York : Springer-Verlag,
c1988.                                      ③  ④              ⑤
⑥       x, 115 p.; ill.; 25cm. -- (Research in criminology)
       ⎧ includes indexes.                              ⑦
⑧      ⎨
       ⎩ Bibliography: p. <101>-107.
SUBJECT HEADINGS (LIBRARY OF CONGRESS; use s=):
       ⎧ Prison psychology.
       ⎪ Prisons--Overcrowding--Psychological aspects.
⑨      ⎨ Crowding stress.
       ⎩ Prisons--United States--Overcrowding.

LOCATION: General Collection (Parks Library) ← ⑩
CALL NUMBER: HV6089 .P38 1988 ← ⑪

TYPE r TO REVISE, h FOR HELP, e FOR SCHOLAR2 INTRODUCTION.
TYPE COMMAND AND PRESS RETURN==>
```

At the top of the screen, SCHOLAR2 will repeat your search and list which record from the set is displayed. Other information you need to locate the book in the Library or to cite it in a bibliography or footnote will be displayed as follows:

1. Author.
2. Title.
3. All of the authors.
4. City of publication.
5. Publisher.

6. Date of publication.
7. Physical description of the book: number of pages, illustrations, height of book, maps, etc.
8. The book has both an index and a bibliography.
9. Library of Congress Subject Headings. These reflect the subject of the book and can be used in a subject search to locate more books on the same topic.
10. Location. This will tell you where the book is located: at the Veterinary Medical Library, Design Reading Room, or General Collection.
11. The Call Number. You must write down this information to locate the book on the shelf.

Commands you may refer to are listed at the bottom of the screen. If you wish to view the next record type **n** <Return>. It is also possible to revise a search. Just type **r** <Return>. The search terms you typed in will appear and you can correct or alter them.

The Author Search

To search for the same book by author, use SCHOLAR2 author searching capability. This is accomplished by typing **A** and the author's name last name, first.

A Paulus Paul

Below is the resulting screen.

```
SCHOLAR2 SEARCH STRATEGY REQUEST: A=PAULUS PAUL
 AUTHOR/TITLE INDEX -- 5 ENTRIES FOUND
    1 LS:PAULUS PAUL B +BASIC GROUP PROCESSES <1983>
    2 LS:PAULUS PAUL B +EFFECT OF PRISON CROWDING ON INMATE BEHAVIOR
         <1981
    3 LS:PAULUS PAUL B +PRISON CROWDING A PSYCHOLOGICAL PERSPECTIVE
         <1988
    4 LS:PAULUS PAUL B +PSYCHOLOGY OF GROUP INFLUENCE <1979
    5 LS:PAULUS PAUL B +PSYCHOLOGY OF GROUP INFLUENCE <1989


TYPE LINE NO. FOR BIBLIOGRAPHIC RECORD WITH CALL NO.
TYPE r TO REVISE, h FOR HELP, e FOR SCHOLAR2 INTRODUCTION
TYPE COMMAND AND PRESS RETURN==>
```

On this screen there are five entries, the books that the Library owns by Paul Paulus. To find the call number and location information, select its line number. For our example, select number **3**, **<Return>**.

The Subject Search

If you are looking for books about prisons but do not know the author or title you can find the same book searching by subject. To search by subject, look up the Library of Congress Subject Heading for your topic. Type in the correct terms as follows.

S prisons--overcrowding

The resulting screen lists two titles.

```
SCHOLAR2 SEARCH REQUEST:  S=PRISONS -OVERCROWDING
 SUBJECT/TITLE INDEX -- 2 TITLES FOUND, 1 - 2 DISPLAYED

PRISONS -OVERCROWDING -PSYCHOLOGICAL ASPECTS
      1 prison crowding: a psychological (1988)LS gen:HV6089 .P38 1988
      2 stress crowding and blood pressu (1987)LS gen:RC451.4.P68 S74 1987




TYPE LINE NO. FOR BIBLIOGRAPHIC RECORD WITH HOLDINGS.
TYPE r TO REVISE, h FOR HELP, e FOR SCHOLAR 2 INTRODUCTION
TYPE COMMAND AND PRESS RETURN==>
```

To view the record for the same book type the number, **1 <Return>**.
The resulting screen you will see will then display same type of information as that shown on the sample screen on page 62.

Looking for Books by Subject

When searching for books by subject many people look up the first term that comes to mind. This works in some cases but not in others. Since English has many synonyms a master list of terms, or subject headings, has been developed to help you locate the materials you need in a catalog. This list is called the *Library of Congress Subject Headings* and consists of three large red books located near the Card Catalog-Subjects and some SCHOLAR2 stations. Below is a sample entry from the *Library of Congress Subject Headings*.

1.		Prisons (May Subd Geog) [HV8301-9920]
2.	UF	Dungeons
		Gaols
		Penal institution
3.	BT	Correctional institution
		Criminal justice, Administration of
4.	RT	Imprisonment
5.	SA	*names of individual prisons*
6.	NT	Arts in prisons
		Death row
		Escapes
7.		-Overcrowding
	UF	Overcrowding of prisons
		Prison overcrowding
	BT	Crowding stress
8.		-Psychiatric care
	USE	Prisoners-Psychiatric care

1. This is the main heading or subject heading.

2. UF means **use for**. Use the term prisons instead of dungeons, gaols, or penal institutions.

3. BT, or Broader Term, refers to a more general term that will include more related material. If you cannot find enough information on a topic, you might try a broader term.

4. RT, Related Term, is another subject heading that has related material on the topic. These may or may not be of use depending on the emphasis of your paper.

5. SA refers to See Also. These are other possible subject headings.

6. NT means Narrower Term. These will be more specific and may be closer to your topic.

7. These are subheadings. These are used to make a broad topic more precise. For example to find information about overcrowding in prisons look under Prisons--overcrowding.

To find books in the Card Catalog-Subjects or in SCHOLAR2 you must identify the right subject heading and use it in the correct form. You will **not** find anything if you look under Overcrowding--prisons. If you have trouble locating a subject heading:

1. Think of synonyms.
2. Ask yourself, is it part of a larger heading? i.e. Prisons--statistics.
3. Could it be more specific such as Crime Prevention rather than Crime and Criminals?
4. Can the phrase be turned around such as Criminal Justice, Administration of?
5. If you need help, ask at the Reference Desk.

It is also possible to look up people as a subject to find information **about** them. This can be particularly helpful when looking for literary criticism about the works of a particular author. When looking for a person as a subject their names are inverted Hellman, Lillian or, on SCHOLAR2, Hellman Lillian.

As you have seen, SCHOLAR2 is a complex and powerful system, but computer searching does have drawbacks. If you misspell a word you will come up with nothing. It is important to know exact titles, authors names, and subject headings when conducting title, author, and subject searches. With a little practice you will become a proficient searcher and be able to locate quickly and efficiently the materials you will need. Remember that if you have any questions or want to learn more about searching you can ask your course instructor or at the Reference Desk.

Keyword Searching

A particularly powerful component of SCHOLAR2 is its ability to perform keyword searching. In keyword searching exact word order in a title or subject is not important. The computer will search for terms wherever they appear in the record. Therefore, if you remember a few words in the title of a book but not the exact title type, for keyword, **K [known title words]** <Return>. SCHOLAR2 will retrieve all the titles, both books and serials, in the database with those words in the title or in any other part of the record. It is also possible for you to do more sophisticated searching using the Boolean logic discussed in Chapter 7.

In addition to using the Boolean operators **and, or,** or **not,** it is also possible to

truncate words using the $ symbol at the end of a word. Truncation allows you to search for various forms of a word at the same time. For example, if you typed in **K train$** you would get books that had both **train** and **trains** in the record. You must use truncation with care, because sometimes the results can be confusing. For instance, should you type in k cat$, not only would you get cat and cats but you would get catalogs, catalytic converters, catatonic, and so on.

Sometimes you may want to use more than one Boolean operator in a search. In those instances you must use parentheses in order to tell the computer what to do first. Suppose you were interested in comparing prison overcrowding in the United States and Great Britain. A possible search would be:

K (United States or Great Britain or England or United Kingdom) and Prison$ and overcrowd$

Enclosed in the parentheses are the two countries and some synonyms for Great Britain in case there are relevant books that use an alternate name. SCHOLAR2 will combine all the entries with those terms in them into one large group. Next it will find all the entries with prison, prisons, prisoners, and so on in the entry and all the entries with terms like overcrowding and overcrowded in them. Finally, it will combine all three and tell you how many books in the Parks Library are about prison overcrowding in Great Britain and the United States. This group could include both comparative works and books about only one of the countries.

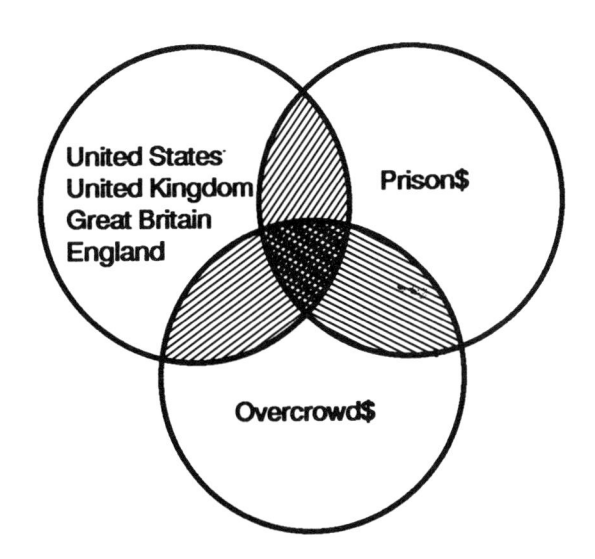

Keyword searching can help alleviate some of the disadvantages of searching by title, author, or subject. You do not need the exact title, author, or subject heading, but it too has disadvantages. Sometimes keyword will retrieve books that are not on your topic because the words entered can have more than one meaning. Sometimes books are missed because the words entered are not in the title.

SCHOLAR2 Screens

Sometimes what would appear to be a straightforward search can become complicated. For example, a search for *Time* magazine,

    T time \<Return\>

results in the following GUIDE screen:

```
SCHOLAR2 SEARCH REQUEST:  T=TIME
 AUTHOR/TITLE GUIDE -- 647 ENTRIES FOUND
  1           TIME <
  93          TIME B
  113         TIME D
  128         TIME E
  176         TIME G
  189         TIME I
  212         TIME L
  247         TIME M
  258         TIME N
  332         TIME P
  344         TIME R
  355         TIME S
  427         TIME T
  492         TIME U
  510         TIMEBE
  520         TIMELI
  614         TIMESC
  636         TIMETI

TYPE NO. OF GUIDE TERM THAT MATCHES OR PRECEDES DESIRED ENTRY TO SEE
INDEX.
TYPE r TO REVISE, h FOR HELP, e FOR SCHOLAR2 INTRODUCTION
TYPE COMMAND AND PRESS RETURN==>
```

SCHOLAR2 came up with 647 citations! Why did it do that? How do you find *Time* magazine in all of those? SCHOLAR2 is programmed to respond with all the titles that **begin** with the words you have entered. 647 refers to the number of titles in the database in which the first word is **time**. This is a **guide screen**, so it does not list complete titles. When SCHOLAR2 finds many entries that match your search it will provide a guide screen. This screen allows you to narrow down or select what you are looking for when you get such a large set. For example, "Time L" in the middle of the screen refers to the first word in the title, Time, and the first letter in the second word, L. Since *Time* is a one word title, look farther up the screen. The first line reads Time<. The <, or carrot, signifies that there are no more words in the title. Type 1, the line number, and <Return> to select *Time*.

    1 \<Return\>

SCHOLAR2 responds with an INDEX screen.

```
SCHOLAR2 SEARCH REQUEST: T=TIME
 AUTHOR/TITLE INDEX -- 647 ENTRIES FOUND, 1 - 18 DISPLAYED
 1 LS:TIME <CHIC
 2 LS:TIME <CHIC MICROFILM
 3 LS:TIME +MAN OF THE YEAR A TIME HONORED TRADITION <1987
 4 LS:TIME +MULLIGATAWNY MEDALLION AND FOUR OTHER SHORT PLAYS <1926
 5 LS:TIME +ELECTRIC LIGHT ORCHESTRA <1981
 6 LS:TIME *GOUDSMIT SAMUEL ABRAHAM <1966
 7 LS:TIME A BIBLIOGRAPHY *KRUDY ELMER S <1976
 8 LS:TIME A PHILOSOPHICAL ANALYSISK *CHAPMAN T <1982
 9 LS:TIME A PHILOSOPHICAL TREATMENT *SEDDON KEITH <1987
10 LS:TIME A TIME AN AUTOBIOGRAPHY *DAVYS SARAH <1971
11 LS:TIME ACTION NECESSITY A PROOF OF FREE WILL *DENYER NICHOLAS <1981
12 LS:TIME AFTER TIME *APPEL ALLEN <1985
13 LS:TIME AFTER TIME *FARRELL M J <1983
14 LS:TIME AFTER TIME* FARRELL M J <1984
15 LS:TIME AGO LOST MORE TALES OF JAHDU *HAMILTON VIRGINIA <1973
16 LS:TIME AGO TALES OF JAHDU *HAMILTON VIRGINIA <1969
17 LS:TIME AMONG THE MAYA TRAVELS IN BELIZE QUATEMALA AND *WRIGHT
      RONALD <1989
18 LS:TIME AND AGAIN *FINNEY JACK <1970

TYPE m FOR MORE ENTRIES. TYPE LINE NO. FOR BIBLIOGRAPHIC RECORD WITH CALL
NO. TYPE g FOR GUIDE. TYPE r TO REVISE, h FOR HELP, e FOR SCHOLAR 2
INTRODUCTION. TYPE COMMAND AND PRESS RETURN==>
```

The **index screen** lists titles beginning with the line you selected. When there is more than one entry with the same title they are listed in chronological order. Notice that at the bottom of the screen there is a list of commands. If you wish to view the next group of titles, or more entries, type **m** <Return>. If you wish to return to the guide screen type **g** <Return>. At the top, lines 1 and 2 both read *Time*; 1 is for the paper copy, 2 is for the microfilm copy. <CHIC is the abbreviation of the city of publication, Chicago. This can help you identify a publication when more than one magazine has the same title. Type **1** <Return> to find out the Library's holdings or what the Library owns; the call numbers, and location information.

```
SCHOLAR2 SEARCH REQUEST:  T=TIME
BIBLIOGRAPHIC RECORD -- NO. 1 OF 647 ENTRIES FOUND

Time. -- Vol. 1, no. 1 (Mar. 3, 1923) -- <Chicago,: Time Inc.>, 1923-
     v. : ill. ; 28 cm.
     Weekly <, Apr. 15, 1985->
     Weekly (except one week a year) <. Dec. 26, 1977->
     Absorbed: Literary digest May 1938
     Imprint varies
     Indexed in its entirety by: Magazine index 1977- Readers' guide to periodical literature
ISSN 034-0464
     Indexed selectively by: ABI/INFORM March 1975-Jan. 1978  Book review index ISSN 0524-0581
Cumulative index to nursing & allied health literature ISSN 0146-5554   Energy information abstracts
ISSN 0147-6758  Hospital literature index
```

This screen gives information about the history of the magazine such as when it began publication. To get more information press <Return>.

```
SCHOLAR SEARCH REQUEST:  T=TIME
BIBLIOGRAPHIC RECORD -- NO. 1 OF 647 ENTRIES FOUND (CONTINUED)

Time ... 1923-   (continued)
ISSN 0018-5736 Infobank Jan. 1969- Media review digest ISSN 0363-7778  Popular
magazine review  ISSN 0740-3763 1984-
     Indexed selectively by: Predicasts
     Special issues accompany some volumes.
     Cumulative indexes.

LOCATION: General Collection (Parks Library)   ← (1)
CALL NUMBER:  AP2  .T48  ← (2)
LIBRARY HAS:
     V. 15-YR. JAN. 1930  ← (3)

LOCATION: PERIODICAL ROOM  ← (1)
CALL NUMBER:  AP2  .T49  ← (2)

          FOR ANOTHER COPY AT THIS OR ANOTHER LOCATION, PRESS RETURN

TYPE n FOR NEXT RECORD.  TYPE i FOR INDEX, g FOR GUIDE.
TYPE r TO REVISE, h FOR HELP, e FOR SCHOLAR2 INTRODUCTION.
TYPE COMMAND AND PRESS RETURN==>
```

On this screen is the location, call number, and holdings information.

1. The bound issues are located in the General Collection and the unbound issues in the Periodical Room.
2. Call number. It is the same regardless of the location.
3. The Library's holdings or the years and volume numbers the Library owns.

The Card Catalog

The Card Catalog is made up of cards filed alphabetically. Catalog cards list a lot of helpful information about each item in the collection. Like SCHOLAR2, the card gives enough information to locate the book in the library and to cite the book in a footnote or bibliography. The Card Catalog can be searched by author, title or subject. Remember, the Card Catalog is divided into two parts; "Authors and Titles" and "Subjects". In order to use the Card Catalog it is necessary to be able to interpret the information on a card. Below is a sample card from the card catalog. You will find that the information provided is the same as on SCHOLAR2 but the arrangement is slightly different.

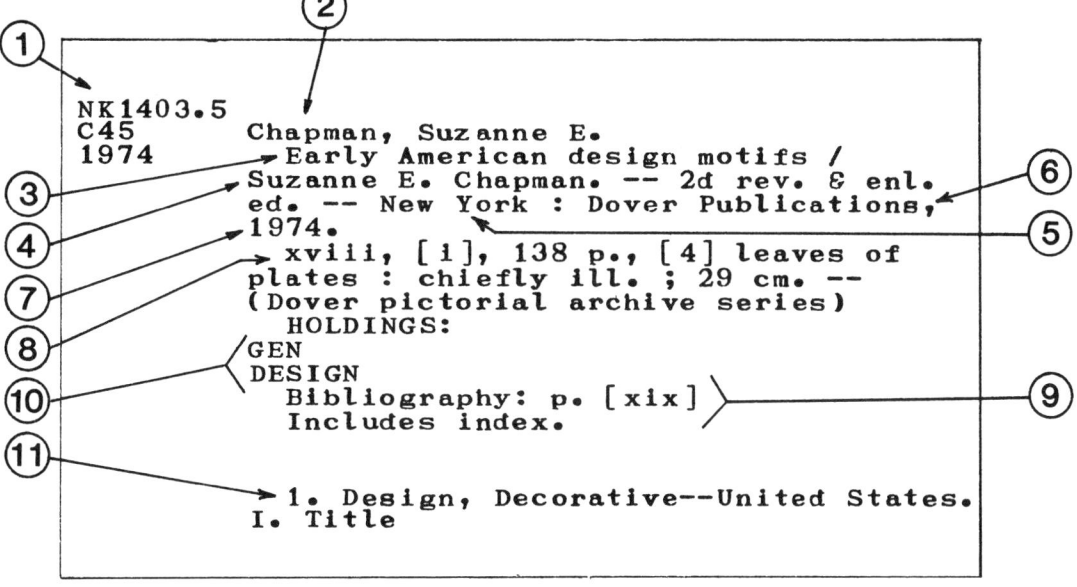

```
NK1403.5
C45      Chapman, Suzanne E.
1974       Early American design motifs /
         Suzanne E. Chapman. -- 2d rev. & enl.
         ed. -- New York : Dover Publications,
         1974.
           xviii, [i], 138 p., [4] leaves of
         plates : chiefly ill. ; 29 cm. --
         (Dover pictorial archive series)
           HOLDINGS:
         GEN
         DESIGN
           Bibliography: p. [xix]
           Includes index.

           1. Design, Decorative--United States.
         I. Title
```

1. Call number.

2. Author.

3. Title.

4. All the authors if the book has more than one.

5. City of publication.

6. Publisher.

7. Year of publication.

8. Physical description of the book. This can include the number of pages, height of the book, maps, illustrations, etc.

9. The book has both a bibliography and an index. If they are not listed on the card in this location then the book does not have them.

10. Holdings information, or what the library owns, is listed here. GEN is the abbreviation for the General Collection and means that there is one copy of the book located in the General Collection. Design is the abbreviation for the Design Reading Room. Other abbreviations used are, REF for the Reference Collection, VET for the Veterinary Medical Library, etc. If you do not understand an abbreviation ask at the Reference Desk. Be sure that you check the location of books that you want. Note that some cards do not list holdings information, in those cases there is one copy of the book located in the General Collection.

11. *Library of Congress Subject Headings* reflect the subject of the book. These cards are filed in the Card Catalog-Subjects for all books purchased through 1988. If a book is helpful to you, you may want to look under these headings for similar material.

Filing Rules

Locating items in the Card Catalog can be confusing. If you follow a few basic rules your search for information can be simplified. For authors and titles use these steps:

1. When there is more than one book by an author they are filed under the author's name and then in alphabetical order by title.

    King, Stephen
    Cujo

    King, Stephen
    Firestarter

    King, Stephen
    Night Shift

2. If a title of a book starts with the same word as an author's last name, the authors' names come before the title cards.

    King, Diana
    King, Stephen
    King, Walter
    King of the Road

3. Articles are ignored if they are the first word in a title but not if they appear within a title.

> *A Last Lamp Burning*
> *The Last Landscape*
> *Last Laugh*
> *Last Man Around the World*
> *Last Man at Arlington*
> *The Last Man in Europe*

4. Abbreviations and numbers are filed as though they were spelled out.

Dr.	Doctor
8	Eight
1984	Nineteen Eighty Four
Mrs.	Mistress
%	Percent
St. Louis	Saint Louis

5. Mc and M' are interfiled with Mac.

Because subject headings can have various forms they are arranged in a precise order in the Card Catalog-Subjects. The following subject headings are in the correct filing order:

Subject Heading	Description
PRISONS	The main subject headings--general works
PRISONS--CONSTRUCTION PRISONS--LAW AND LEGISLATION	Subject subdivided by form or topic
PRISONS--IOWA PRISONS--UNITED STATES	Subject subdivided by geographic location
PRISONS, COEDUCATIONAL PRISONS, MUSIC IN	Inverted heading
PRISONS AND RACE RELATIONS PRISONS IN LITERATURE	Phrase heading

Serials Catalog

The *ISU Serials Catalog* is the third catalog available in the Library. To determine if the Iowa State University Library holds the periodical title, you want, you will need to check either SCHOLAR2 or the *ISU Serials Catalog*; however, at present the *ISU Serials Catalog* is the easier of the two to use. In this catalog, all the serials, newspapers, magazines, journals that the Library holds are listed alphabetically by title.

This catalog is a computer-generated set of two red volumes labeled *ISU Serials Catalog--Titles*. In the second volume, following the Zs, is a section with blue pages listing the corporate bodies that publish titles included in the *ISU Serials Catalog*. Copies of the *ISU Serials Catalog* can be found on each floor and tier as well as in the service areas of the Library. There are also multiple copies available in the Reference Area and around the Card Catalog. Some sets include a loose-leaf supplement that provides the most recent additions and corrections.

If this Library owns a periodical title, it will be listed in the *ISU Serials Catalog*; however, the Library does not have all the periodicals indexed in all the indexes. If you do not find the title you are looking for, either the Library does not have it or you have not looked in the right place. In addition, sometimes the Library has some, but not all, issues of a periodical for which there is an entry in the *ISU Serials Catalog*.

Following are a few of the important rules to help you locate a title in the *ISU Serials Catalog*:

1. Disregard articles (a, an, the), prepositions (of, on, at, to, for, from, over) and punctuation (-, ., :) **within** the title. These titles are in the correct order.

    Journal of Advertising Research
    Journal of the American Veterinary Medical Association
    Journal - Institute of Animal Technicians
    Journal of Research in Music Education
    The Journal of Special Education
    Journals of the Continental Congress

2. Numbers come before letters and are **not** alphabetized as if spelled out.

    60 Minutes   *National 4-H News*
    A.V. Guide   *National Aircraft Standards*

3. Initials are alphabetized as if they were words of one letter. All abbreviations are alphabetized as printed, not as if spelled out.

> *U.S. News and World Report*
> *Uganda Journal*
> *United States Law Week*

If you still can't find what you're looking for, consider these other possibilities. Is the spelling correct? Do you have the right ending on the first word? If there are initials in the title, did you look for them as words of one letter or as an acronym?

Another possibility is that there is a corporate body such as an organization or government agency in the title. Did you use the Corporate Body Index? For example, if you're looking for a serial publication from the corporate body, American Physical Education Association, look in the Corporate Body Index of the *ISU Serials Catalog*. You will find this entry:

```
AMERICAN PHYSICAL EDUCATION ASSOCIATION.
   JOURNAL OF HEALTH, PHYSICAL EDUCATION, RECREATION.
   GV201  .J826
   RESEARCH QUARTERLY - AMERICAN ALLIANCE FOR HEALTH,
   PHYSICAL EDUCATION AND RECREATION.   GV201  .AM35R
   SEARCH ALSO UNDER-- AMERICAN ASSOCIATION FOR HEALTH
   AND PHYSICAL EDUCATION.
   SEE ALSO-- AMERICAN ASSOCIATION FOR HEALTH, PHYSICAL
   EDUCATION, AND RECREATION.
   SEE ALSO-- AMERICAN ALLIANCE FOR HEALTH, PHYSICAL
   EDUCATION, RECREATION, AND DANCE.
```

The title of this publication is *Journal of Health, Physical Education, Recreation* and must be located in the title section of the *ISU Serials Catalog* to get complete information about its holdings and location.

You can use the *ISU Serials Catalog* to determine if this Library has an article cited in *Business Periodicals Index*:

> **Advertising**
> *See also*
>   Creativity in advertising
>   Deceptive advertising
>   Direct mail advertising
>   Direct response advertising
>   Display of merchandise
> Advertising: art, science, or business? L. Bogart. *J Advert Res* 28:47-52 D '88-Ja '89
> PR on the offensive: we can do better than ads [marketing mix] D. Edelman. *Advert Age* 60:20 Mr 13 '89
> Stoking the engine of the economy. D. F. Helm, Jr. *Mark Commun* 12:48 N '87
>
>   **Credibility**
> *See also*
>   Deceptive advertising
> Ad reporters exploit pull of the press [taking advantage of credibility of real reporter] P. Winters. *Advert Age* 59:30 Ap 4 '88

To read this article, you will need to use the *ISU Serials Catalog* to determine if this Library has the *Journal of Advertising Research* and if so, where it is shelved. Once you find the *Journal of Advertising Research* in the *ISU Serials Catalog*, the entry looks like this:

```
JOURNAL OF ADVERTISING RESEARCH
    V.1- ; 1960-
       HF5801 .J826
       GEN; 1-16, (17), 18-; 1960-; EXCEPT CURRENT
                         ISSUES
       PER;   CURRENT ISSUES
```

Following is a line-by-line explanation of this entry:

    v.1- ; 1960-   **Publication record**

    Journal of Advertising Research began publication with volume 1 for 1960, and it continues to be published to the present date as indicated by the (-).

    HF5801 .J826   **Call Number**

    Notice the call number is written entirely on one line and is the most indented line.

    GEN; 1-16, (17), 18-; 1960-; EXCEPT CURRENT ISSUES
                                                    Location; Holdings

    In the General Collection, you will find all the bound volumes of *Journal of Advertising Research* beginning with volume 1 for 1960, except for 17, which the ( ) indicate is partially missing, and the current issues.

    PER;   CURRENT ISSUES   **Location; Holdings**

    The recent unbound or current issues, back approximately one year, are in the Periodical Room.

    The bound volumes in the General Collection and the current, unbound issues in the Periodical Room make up a set of the *Journal of Advertising Research* that is complete except for some issue or issues in volume 17, which are missing. The June 20, 1988 issue of volume 59 is not within the latest one year; therefore, it will be in the General Collection. To locate this volume, check the Call Number Locations Guide, which indicates that the HF call numbers are located on floor 3. Anytime you do not understand an abbreviation or symbol, turn to the front of the *ISU Serials Catalog* for an explanation. The list on the next page shows some of the codes and locations also that appear in the front of the *ISU Serials Catalog*.

CODE	LOCATIONS
Design	Design Reading Room, 111 Design Building
Econ	Economics/Sociology Reading Room, 368 Heady Hall
MATH	Mathematics Reading Room, 401 Carver Hall
MICRO	Microforms Center, 140 Parks Library
MUSIC	Music Department, Music Hall
PHYS SCI	Physical Sciences Reading Room, 217 Office and Lab Building
VET	Veterinary Medical Library, 2280 College of Veterinary Medicine

Many publications are shelved permanently in these locations around the campus and are considered part of the Library's holdings.

The Library may have additional copies of a periodical shelved in different locations or formats. For example:

```
ART IN AMERICA
    V. 1- ; 1913-
        N1 .AR76
    GEN; 1-57, (58), 59-; 1913-; EXCEPT CURRENT
                                  ISSUES
    PER;    CURRENT ISSUES
    DESIGN;   LATEST 3 YEARS
        FOR ADDITIONAL HOLDINGS SEE FOLLOWING RECORD.
ART IN AMERICA.
    V. 1- ; 1913-
    TITLE VARIES: DEC. 1921-APR. 1939, ART IN AMERICA AND
    ELSEWHERE.
        N1 .AR76 MICROFILM
    MICRO; 53-; 1965-
        FOR ADDITIONAL HOLDINGS SEE PREVIOUS RECORD.
```

If you wish to read the most recent issue of *Art in America*, you should be able to find it in both the Periodical Room and the Design Reading Room. Note that there are two separate entries for *Art in America* because it is available in both print and nonprint, or microform, formats. If you need to use a volume that is more than three years old, you need to go to the Microform Center or use the Call Number Locations Guide to determine where the "N" call numbers are located in the General Collection.

In other instances the Library may not have a single complete set of a periodical. For example, the *Journal of Management Studies* began publishing with volume 1 in 1964, but we began receiving the journal in 1982 with volume 19. Remember, the information that applies to the volumes available appears beneath the call number, which is always the most indented line.

Another situation that may prevent you from finding a periodical is a title change. For example, *Architectural Preservation Forum*, volume 1, was published under this title and then continued under the title *The Forum; Bulletin of the Committee on Preservation*.

```
ARCHITECTURAL PRESERVATION FORUM.
    V. 1, NO. 1-2; FEB.-DEC. 1979//
    CONTINUED BY: THE FORUM; BULLETIN OF THE COMMITTEE ON
    PRESERVATION.
        NA106 .A72X
      DESIGN; 1; 1979
```

```
THE FORUM; BULLETIN OF THE COMMITTEE ON PRESERVATION.
    V. 2- ; JUNE 1980-
        NA106 .A721X
      DESIGN; 2-; 1980-
```

Understanding how to use a library's catalogs and knowing what each one contains will make looking for information in any library easier and more efficient.

APPENDIX A

Iowa State University Library

Educational Objectives

Locating, Interpreting, and Using Information

Iowa State University defines its mission to be "the discovery and dissemination of new knowledge by supporting research, scholarship and creative activity." The University's goal is to "instill in its students the discernment, intellectual curiosity, knowledge and skills essential for their individual development and their useful contribution to society."[1] The achievement of this goal requires that our students know how to find and use information. Research and scholarship depend upon a knowledge base, a recognition of the need for sufficient evidence before drawing conclusions and the belief that application, analysis and synthesis of information underlie thoughtful judgement.

These concepts should be a part of each student's experience. Teaching the value of information in the scholarly process is the responsibility of the entire Iowa State University faculty. The Library faculty bear particular responsibility for initiating the integration of this value throughout the University curriculum, becoming partners with their classroom colleagues. This process of integration is recognized in a national report as essential to the provision of a quality undergraduate education. College: The Undergraduate Experience in America recommends that for students to become independent self-directed learners "All undergraduates should be introduced carefully to the full range of resources for learning on a campus. They should be given bibliographic instruction and be encouraged to spend at least as much time in the library - using its wide range of resources - as they spend in classes."[2]

The objectives outlined in the document define what we anticipate all students would achieve by the end of their educational career at Iowa State University. It is our hope that students will learn to use all libraries with ease, confident of their information-seeking skills.

Objective A: Students understand what information is and its value in both scholarly and practical processes.

I. Students recognize the need for information when approaching a problem or an issue.

   A. They realize that sufficient evidence is needed before drawing conclusions.
   B. They understand that knowledge is divided into specific areas or disciplines.
   C. They are aware that there are a variety of information sources, including published, electronic and personal communication.

II. Students recognize that libraries organize knowledge.

   A. They understand that learning how to use libraries is an integral part of education.
   B. They know that libraries offer many different types of services.
   C. They realize that these basic skills are transferable among libraries and can be applied to future learning situations.

III. Students know that libraries provide multiple kinds of information.

   A. They are aware of the various physical formats in which information may be found, such as print, microform, videotape, map, manuscript, electronic database, or computer disc.
   B. They understand the difference between monographs and serials.
   C. They are aware of types of sources available for their research, including primary, secondary, and tertiary.
   D. They are able to distinguish between popular and scholarly materials.

Objective B: Students understand standard systems for the organization of information and have the capability to retrieve information from a variety of systems.

I. Students understand general research strategies used to obtain information.

   A. They are able to focus topics, analyze problem statements and seek information.
   B. They are able to ask questions that will obtain needed information.
   C. They are able to use reference materials such as encyclopedias, dictionaries, bibliographies, directories, and handbooks related to their discipline or subject area.

II. Students are aware of and able to use the appropriate sources and library services in order to locate needed information.

   A. They are aware of and able to use the appropriate finding aids in order to locate needed information.
   B. Students are able to physically locate information.

---

[1] "Iowa State University - A Statement of Mission," November 1988.
[2] Ernest L. Boyer, College: The Undergraduate Experience in America, (New York: Harper and Row, 1987), page 165.

APPENDIX B

BIBLIOGRAPHY

As students you are often required to submit a bibliography as part of a class report or term paper. A bibliography is a means of giving credit to the sources which you have used in writing your paper and avoid using the work of another without giving them credit which is plagiarism. Citations should be complete so that anyone using your information could find the same source again. By providing a good bibliography, you are crediting those works which shaped your research. The bibliography can be a list of the sources relating to a specific subject as shown in the following example, or a list of works by one author. The bibliography may contain citations to different types of materials such as books, serials, government publications or reference books such as encyclopedias. It may also contain citations to personal interviews, or any other type of source used in constructing your project or paper. In addition, the bibliography gives your reader a quick way to check the range and type of sources you have used in your research.

How this information is actually cited is determined by the style that is used to convey the information. There are several style manuals available, but often your instructor will assign you to use a particular one. If none is assigned, ask at the Reference Desk. The style manual used to prepare the bibliography on **acid rain** on page 82 is *A Manual for Writers of Term Papers, Theses, and Dissertations* by Kate Turabian and often referred to as simply Turabian. Following is a list of the most commonly used style manuals, all of which are available at the Reference Desk.

American Psychological Association. *Publication Manual of the American Psychological Association*. 3rd ed. Washington, D.C.: American Psychological Association, 1983.

This authoritative manual is commonly referred to as APA, and is widely used in psychology and other social sciences.

CBE Style Manual Committee. *Council of Biology Editors Style Manual: A Guide for Authors, Editors and Publishers in the Biological Sciences*. 4th ed. Arlington, VA: Conference of Biological Editors, Inc., 1978.

This style manual is widely used in the biological sciences.

The Chicago Manual of Style. 13th edition. Chicago: University of Chicago Press, 1982.

    This is a comprehensive guide to the forms and formats governing the written presentation of research. This manual can answer questions about abbreviations, spelling, or grammatical style. This is the reference book that professional editors keep next to the dictionary. Other style manuals are often based on this one.

Gibaldi, Joseph and Walter S. Achtert. *The MLA Handbook for Writers of Research Papers*. 3rd ed. New York: Modern Language Association of America, 1988.

    The "MLA Style" is most commonly used in the humanities and foreign language fields. The many sections of this book contain information on everything from selecting a topic to taking notes and using quotations.

Turabian, Kate L. *Student's Guide for Writing College Papers*. 5th ed. Chicago: University of Chicago Press, 1987.

    This standard style lists almost every conceivable type of footnote and bibliography entry and provides several extensive bibliographies of reference books and other reference sources. This is the style being used in the bibliography and examples which follow.

If you don't know which style manual to use, ask at the Reference Desk.

BIBLIOGRAPHY

Acid Rain: Requiem or Recovery? 27 min., distributed by National Film Board of Canada, 1983. Videocassette.

"Administration's clean air plan called 'new era in environmental protection'." JAPCA 39 (July 1989): 988-89.

Barth, H., ed. Reversibility of acidification. New York: Elsevier Applied Science, 1987.

Congressional Budget Office. Curbing acid rain: cost, budget, and coal-market effects, by Marc Chupka. Washington D.C.: GPO, 1986.

Kete, Nancy, Diane H. Brown and Randy A. Roig. Acid rain control legislation: costs to Maryland electric utilities and implementation. Annapolis, Md.: The Program, 1985.

McGraw-Hill Encyclopedia of Science and Technology, 1987 ed. S.v. "Acid Rain."

Metcalfe, S.E. and R.G. Derwent. "Geographical research on acid rain: modeling acid deposition and the possible effects of emission controls." Geographical Journal 155 (November 1989): 366-377.

Parker, H.D. and G.D. Pitt. Pollution control instrumentation for oil and effluents. Boston: Graham and Trotman, 1987.

"Philip R. Sharp discusses the importance of and the inequities in President Bush's acid rain legislation." Washington Post. 22 June 1989, p.27.

Postel, Sandra. Air pollution, acid rain, and the future of forests. Washington D.C.: Worldwatch Institute, 1984.

Sagan, Carl. Interview by the personal author, 23 April 1990.

Transboundary air pollution: effects and control: report prepared with the framework of the Convention on Long-range Transboundary Air Pollution. New York: United Nations. 1986.

Wilcher, Marshal E. The politics of acid rain. Brookfield, Mass.: Avebury, 1988.

APPENDIX C
SELECTED INDEXING SERVICES

GENERAL

Des Moines Register Index (alphabetical)
　　An index to a daily newspaper published in Des Moines, Iowa, which contains standard news coverage of Iowa as well as in-depth reporting for agriculture, and politics. (online, microfiche, print)

Magazine Index (alphabetical)
　　An index to popular magazine covering general subjects such as current events, leisure time activities, home center arts, sports, recreation, consumer product evaluations, and views pro- con issues. (microfilm)

National Newspaper Index (alphabetical)
　　An index to the *New York Times, Wall Street Journal, Christian Science Monitor,* and *Washington Post.* (microfilm)

Readers' Guide to Periodical Literature (alphabetical)
　　This popular index includes references to periodical journals of a general and non-technical nature. Entry is by author, title, and subject. (print or CD-ROM)

AGRICULTURAL AND BIOLOGICAL SCIENCES

AGRICOLA
　　The *Bibliography of Agriculture* from the National Agricultural Library is the database for this indexing services. It indexes current publications in agriculture published throughout the world. (CD-ROM)

Biological and Agricultural Index (alphabetical)
　　An excellent and easily used index in the biological and agricultural sciences, this index covers such topics as animal sciences, biology, botany, ecology, entomology, genetics, mycology, agricultural economics, and engineering. (print)

General Science Index (alphabetical)
　　This index to periodical articles includes such field as astronomy, atmospheric science, biology, botany, chemistry, earth science, environment and conservation, food and nutrition, genetics, mathematics, medicine and health, microbiology, physics, physiology, psychology, and zoology. (print)

Index Veterinarius (alphabetical)
   This is a comprehensive index of world literature in veterinary medicine and related areas. The dictionary arrangement of references by subject and authors is in two separate sections. There is a separate listing of books, reviews, and reports. (print)

Nutrition Abstracts and Reviews (numerical)
   Nutrition Abstracts and Reviews is published into two parts: *Part A--Human and Experimental* and *Part B--Livestock, Feeds and Fertilizers*. Coverage includes such areas as chemical composition of foodstuffs, human diet, vitamins, radiation, and feeding of animals. (print)

ARCHITECTURE AND ENGINEERING

Applied Science and Technology Index (alphabetical)
   This index covers a wide range of scientific and technical subjects including engineering, chemistry, physics, transportation, geology, automation, and food technology. (print and CD-ROM)

Avery Index to Architectural Periodicals (alphabetical)
   This index is based on architectural collection at Columbia University and is updated annual. It includes articles in the fine arts, housing and city planning. (print)

Engineering Index (numerical)
   This index is international in scope, covering over 2700 serials which include publications of societies, and papers from conferences. (print)

BUSINESS AND ECONOMICS

Business Index (alphabetical)
   This index covers such business periodicals as *Business Week, Wall Street Journal, Forbes,* and *Barron's.* (microfilm)

Business Periodicals Index (alphabetical)
   This is an easily used subject index to periodicals in such fields as accounting, advertising, banking and finance, insurance, labor and management, and taxation. (print and CD-ROM)

Journal of Economic Literature (numerical)
   This indexes articles from the principle economic journals of various countries. It is arranged by detailed classification scheme. (print)

Predicast F & S Index: United States (numerical)
   Indexes articles and information from the trade magazines, the financial periodicals including *ValueLine*, and the economic periodicals. (print)

COMPUTER SCIENCE AND MATH

ACM Guide to Computing Literature (numerical)
   An index to books, journal articles, conference proceedings, technical reports for all fields of computer science and its application. (print)

Applied Science and Technology Index (alphabetical)
   This index covers a wide range of scientific and technical subjects including computer science, engineering, chemistry, physics, transportation, geology, automation, and food technology. (print)

Mathematical Reviews (numerical)
   An index to the pure and the applied mathematical literature. It is arranged by the American Mathematical Society's Subject Classification Scheme. (print)

EDUCATION AND PSYCHOLOGY

Education Index (alphabetical)
   A basic index to the educational literature. (print)

ERIC: Educational Resources Information Center
   This is the database for the education literature which includes both CIJE (journals) and RIE (documents). (CD-ROM)

   CIJE: Current Index to Journal in Education (numerical)
   This is one of a number of ERIC indexing services. It is an index to the current periodical literature in education, covering approximately 750 major educational and education-related journals. (print)

   RIE: Resources in Education (numerical)
   This is one of a number of ERIC indexing services. It is an index to "documents" in education. The documents cited are available on microfiche in the Parks Library Microform Center. (print)

Physical Education Index (alphabetical)
   This index includes both U.S. and foreign periodicals . It covers such subjects as dance, health, physical education, physical therapy, recreation, sports, and sports medicine as well as biographies of outstanding professionals. (print)

Psychological Abstracts (alphabetical)
　　This is an excellent indexing service in the area of any of the behavioral sciences. It abstracts new books, official documents, dissertations, periodical articles. (print)

GOVERNMENT, LAW, AND POLITICAL SCIENCE

CIS/ Annual (numerical)
　　This is an index to the publications of the United States Congress prepared by the Congressional Information Services. A detailed index, provides access to brief abstracts of prints, hearings, documents, reports, and special reports. (print)

MARCIVE
　　An index to United States government documents. (CD-ROM)

Public Affairs Information Service. Bulletin. (P.A.I.S.) (alphabetical)
　　This is a subject index to books, pamphlets, periodical articles, government documents and other materials in sociology, economics, public policy, trade, and public affairs. The emphasis is on factual and statistical information. (print)

HUMANITIES

America: History and Life (numerical)
　　An index to articles on the history of the United States and Canada. It is issued in four parts. The subject index is Part D and the articles with citations and abstracts are in Part A. (print)

Art Index (alphabetical)
　　This index searches 150 periodicals, including foreign journals and museum bulletins; some of the subject are archeology, architecture, photography and films, art history, and landscape design. (print)

Humanities Index (alphabetical)
　　Indexing American, Canadian, and British periodicals, this publication includes references to reviews of films, plays, short stories, and poems plus a special section at the back for references to book reviews. Some of the subjects included are archeology, broadcasting, dance, film, journalism, literature, music, philosophy, and religion. (print)

MLA International Bibliography of Books and Articles (alphabetical)
　　Indexes articles and books in modern languages and modern literature. It is arranged in five parts with a separate subject index. (print and CD-ROM)

Music Index (alphabetical)
An index to current music periodical literature. It includes reviews of musical performances, recordings, and books. (print)

PHYSICAL SCIENCES

General Science Index (alphabetical)
This index to periodical articles includes such fields as astronomy, atmospheric science, biology, botany, chemistry, earth sciences, environment and conservation, food and nutrition, genetics, mathematics, medicine and health, microbiology, physics, physiology, psychology, and zoology. (print)

SOCIAL SCIENCES

Communication Abstracts (numerical)
This abstracting service covers major communications-related articles, reports, and books from a variety of publishers, research institutions, and information sources. It provides coverage of recent literature in the areas of general communication, mass communication, advertising and marketing, broadcasting, journalism, public relations, radio, public opinion, speech, and television. (print)

Social Sciences Index (alphabetical)
This is an easily used indexing service including references in the fields of anthropology, archeology, economics, environmental, folklore, and sociology. Reviews of books are referenced in a section following the main body of the index. (print and CD-ROM)

APPENDIX D

SELECTED REFERENCE SOURCES

Dictionaries, collected biographies, atlases, almanacs, yearbooks, directories, and encyclopedias are examples of reference materials that contain information commonly needed. A brief description of the kind of information found in some of these volumes may help you choose the appropriate one when the need arises. When using these reference materials for the first time, you may find the how-to-use instructions, given at the front of the volume, helpful.

DICTIONARIES

Oxford English Dictionary
   This is the most comprehensive English dictionary in the world. It is a multi-volume set that traces the development of each word from its first published use to its present usage.

Webster's Third New International Dictionary
   This is an unabridged dictionary which contains about a half million words with detailed information given for each entry.

Webster's New Collegiate Dictionary
   This is an abridged dictionary with only about 150,000 words. If you simply need to check the spelling, pronunciation, or meaning of a word, an abridged dictionary will suffice.

Subject-related Dictionaries
   Most areas of study have dictionaries that define words as they are used in that field. These include medicine, education, music, law, and many other areas of study. These dictionaries are located in the Reference Collection.

COLLECTIVE BIOGRAPHIES

Biography and Genealogy Master Index, 1981-85 Cumulation
   This is an index to biographical sources and in invaluable for locating information about people.

Biography Index

This is a cumulative index to biographical material in selected books and magazines. It is published by the H. W. Wilson company and is used like *Readers' Guide to Periodical Literature*.

Who's Who in America

This standard dictionary of biography briefly describes prominent, living Americans. Entries include personal, educational, and career information. *Who's Who* is the British counterpart.

Current Biography Yearbook

This is published monthly with annual cumulations and includes prominent and newsworthy women and men in the world today, such as authors, political figures, journalists, movie and television stars.

ATLASES

National Atlas of the United States (U.S. Geological Survey)

This atlas is designed to be of practical use to those needing to visualize countrywide distributional patterns and relationships between environmental factors and human activities.

National Geographic Atlas of the World

This atlas presents general reference political maps with descriptions of each country written with the help of prominent geographers, economists and historians. It includes current economic and political data as well as a special section on astronomy and earth sciences.

Rand McNally Commercial Atlas and Marketing Guide

Devoted almost entirely to the United States, this is probably the most detailed atlas of this country. State maps are accompanied by considerable statistical information on marketing and commercial activity of important retail centers and metropolitan trading areas. This atlas is published and revised annually.

ALMANACS AND YEARBOOKS

World Almanac

This almanac contains concise statistics on almost any subject you can think of such as sports, theater, famous people, finance, government, agriculture, trade, and commerce. The texts of some major laws and other important public documents, including the *Constitution of the United States*, are also given. Its excellent, detailed index is at the front of this volume.

Statistical Abstract of the United States

This is an annual summary of national data collected by agencies of the federal government, private agencies, and some states. Grouped by years, the statistical tables cover the subjects of population, vital statistics, climate, social insurance and welfare services, education, elections, agriculture, banking and finance, and comparative international statistics.

Europa Year Book

This is a two-volume annual publication including descriptions of international organizations such as the United Nations and the Nobel Foundation. It also includes statistical surveys of the countries of Europe, Asia, Africa, Australia, and the Americas followed by information on politics, government, religion, education, finance, trade, and the press.

Facts on File

This weekly publication summarizes national and foreign news events, providing an up-to-date source of information on current events. A single volume incorporating these weekly summaries is published annually.

DIRECTORIES

Encyclopedia of Associations

This directory gives brief descriptions of business, commercial, agricultural, social, governmental, legal, scientific, cultural, medical, and religious associations, societies, councils, and organizations along with their addresses and phone numbers.

Official Congressional Directory

This directory contains information of political interest including biographies of U.S. senators and representatives and their Washington, D.C. addresses, membership of congressional committees, personnel of federal departments and agencies, members of the foreign service, and the diplomatic and consular offices in and out of this country.

Iowa Official Register

This register, published every two years, is the official factbook about the State of Iowa. It lists state senators, representatives, committees and departments, county officers, state institutions, elections, and newspapers. Brief biographical information is given about each member of the state legislature. Most of the 50 states publish a register similar to this one.

ENCYCLOPEDIAS

General Encyclopedias

These encyclopedias treat comprehensively all the various branches of knowledge and are usually composed of individual articles arranged alphabetically by subject. Some general encyclopedia titles available in the Reference Collection include: *Encyclopedia Americana, Collier's Encyclopedia, Encyclopedia Britannica*, and *Academic American Encyclopedia*. This last title is also available in CD-ROM format and is called Grolier Electronic Encyclopedia.

Subject Encyclopedias

Virtually every area of study has an encyclopedia composed of articles on subjects relevant to that area. These encyclopedias may consist of only one volume or they may be multi-volume sets. Either way they are usually arranged alphabetically by subject. Some examples of the many subject encyclopedias available in the Reference Collection include: *Encyclopedia of Psychology, Encyclopedia of Religion and Ethics, Encyclopedia of Historic Places, Encyclopedia of Social Sciences, Encyclopedia of Crime and Justice, Encyclopedia of Education, Encyclopedia of World Art, Encyclopedia of World Drama, McGraw-Hill Encyclopedia of Science and Technology*, and the *Encyclopedia of Bioethics*.

APPENDIX E - Library Use Self-Help Questions
Answers to these questions are found on pages 106-109.

<u>Locations and Services</u>

Where would you go to accomplish each of the following? Write the appropriate letter on the line provided.

1. _____ Listen to an audiocassette tape
2. _____ Find U.S. Government Census for 1980
3. _____ Locate a rare book in the Library's Collection
4. _____ Obtain help about where to find a library service
5. _____ Browse through the latest books acquired by the Library
6. _____ Check out a book
7. _____ Read an article placed on reserve by a professor
8. _____ Find a topographic map of Iowa
9. _____ Obtain and read a microfiche
10. _____ View a videotape for class
11. _____ Find the latest available issue of the *New York Times*
12. _____ Obtain assistance in finding information for a term paper
13. _____ Determine if a book is checked out

a. Circulation

b. Reference

c. Information Desk

d. New Book Reading Room

e. Map Room

f. Special Collections

g. Media

h. Reserve

i. Microforms

j. Periodical Room

k. Leisure Reading Room

14. ____ The Periodical Room contains:
   a. All the periodicals in this library.
   b. Only current (unbound) issues of all the periodicals in this library.
   c. Only current (unbound) issues of some of the periodicals in this library.

Locating Publications

Location of Call Numbers

15. Use the Call Number Locations on page (?) to determine the location of the call numbers beginning with the following letters:

   a. QA ____   c. BF ____   e. ISU ____
   b. HD ____   d. SD ____   f. PR ____

Circulation Print-out

```
TX140      R39H                        478-34-5639   2-24
TX140      R39H3                    2  RESERVE(C)    5-13
TX145      G42H       1903            484-52-4688   12-17
TX145      N532M4                  2  250-04-5812    5-13
TX147      C77        1978            LEISURE        5-13
TX147      M28                        LEISURE        5-13
TX147      M451H                      RESERVE(C)     5-13
TX147      R272E                   1  499-66-6531    5-13
TX147      W45                        479-82-9684    3-04
TX147      W75        1973         2  506-84-0722    3-03
```

16. Using this sample above from the Circulation Print-out, answer the following questions.

   a. Is TX147 .W5 checked out? _____

   b. When is TX140 .R39H3 due back to the Library? _____

   c. Where can you locate TX140 R39H3? _____

   d. Is TX147 .M28 checked out? _____ If "no," where can it be located?
   _____

   e. If you need TX147 .R27E before the date it is due, what can you do to obtain it before that date?
   _____

Call Number Sequence

17. In each pair of call numbers below, which would be first on the shelf, **1** or **2**?

	1	2		1	2
a.	T601 R4	TA7 B19	c.	SF601 C29	SF72 D9
b.	DA1411 M6	DA1411 M221 1986	d.	LC4306 G2	LC3 G2

18. Listed below are call numbers in the correct order as they would be arranged on the shelf.

<u> 1 </u> QA21   <u> 2 </u> QA21   <u> 3 </u> QA312   <u> 4 </u> QA312   <u> 5 </u> QA4819
        C14   C21   L34   L34   R92
                                                                  R1

In which space (1,2,3,4,5) should you expect to find the following call numbers? A space can be used more than once.

a. QA72 ____   c. QA4819 .C2 ____   e. QA21.4 ____
   A16   B9

b. QA21 ____   d. QA9 ____   f. Q6302 ____
   C3   R11   T9

19. a. ____ Publications, both books and serials, are arranged on the shelf by (1) call number; (2) author; (3) title.

b. ____ The General Collection includes (1) books only; (2) serials only; (3) both books and serials.

c. ____ The classification system that is used for assigning call numbers in this library is (1) Dewey Decimal; (2) Library of Congress.

d. ____ The first letter(s) and number of a call number are assigned on the basis of (1) author; (2) title; (3) subject.

Indexing Services

Locate a copy of the *Guide to Indexing Services* in the Reference Area to answer questions 20 and 21.

20. Use the Subject Section titled *Guide to Indexing Services* and give two indexing services covering the subject **graphic arts**.

   a. _____   b. _____

21. Using the Title Section of the same list, *Guide to Indexing Services*, give the location of the following indexing services.

   a. *Bibliography of Agriculture* _____

   b. *Sage Urban Studies Abstracts* _____

22. Using the example from *Education Index* on the right, answer the following questions:

   a. How are the references arranged in this indexing service? (alphabetically or numerically)

   _____

   b. What are **Play technique, Playground ball,** and **Playgrounds, School**?

   _____

   c. List two subheadings under the subject **Playgrounds**.

   _____

   _____

```
PLAY technique
    Elementary school counseling with unstruc-
      tured play media. R. C. Nelson. Personnel
      & Guid J 45:24-7 S '66
    Play and discussion. J. R. Suchman. diag
      Instr 76:33+ F '67
    Role of anxiety and cognitive factors in
      children's play behavior. J. B. Gilmore.
      bibliog Child Develop 37:397-416 Je '66
PLAY within a play. See Drama—Technique
PLAYGROUND ball
    Games to improve skills; lead up to softball.
      J. Kautz. Instr 75:38 Je '66
    In and out softball. T. O'Rourke. J Health
      Phys Ed Rec 37:60 My '66
PLAYGROUNDS
            Activities
    If you're working at summer playground.
      camp. il Instr 75:79-80 Je '66
         Great Britain
    Adventure on the Downs. il Times Ed Sup
      2675:394 Ag 26 '66
PLAYGROUNDS, School
    Schools and city save by shared playground
      costs. R. Poteet and G. Schrader. plan Na-
      tions Sch 78:61 S '66
           Equipment
    Challenge a child at play; a learning exper-
      ience. A. B. Etkes. il Am Sch Bd J 153:
      26-8 Ag '66
```

d. What is the information in the block called?

_____

```
                    Equipment
Challenge a child at play: a learning exper-
ience.  A. B. Etkes. il Am Sch Bd J 153:
26-8 Ag '66
```

e. Using the information in the block, identify the following:

1. Title of the article _____

_____

2. Author _____

3. Periodical Title (abbreviated)_____

4. Volume _____

5. Pages _____ 6. Date _____

7. Are there illustrations in the article?_____

Below is an example from *Communication Abstract*.

Advertising Deception, 154, 404, 457,

457

Harris, R. J. et al. Training consumers about misleading advertising: transfer of training and effects of specialized knowledge. Leigh, J. H. and Martin, C. R., Jr., eds. Current issues & research in advertising 1981. Ann Arbor: Graduate School of Business Administration, The University of Michigan, 1981, pp. 105-122.

ADVERTISING DECEPTION. ADVERTISING EFFECTS. CONSUMER BEHAVIOR.

Two experiments were performed to train subjects not to interpret or remember implied product claims in simulated radio advertisements as directly asserted facts. To investigate the effects of specialized knowl-

23. Is this a citation to (a) a journal article; (b) a book; (c) chapter of a book?
    _____

24. Identify the parts of the example on the previous page.

    a. subject heading_____

    b. publisher_____

    c. author(s) of chapter_____

    d. title of chapter_____

    e. editor(s)_____

    f. title of book_____

    g. date_____

    h. pages_____

    i. first line of abstract_____

    _____

25. Using the reference below from *Psychological Abstracts* identify the parts.

    > 2058. **Perry, Cheryl L. & Duke, Daniel L.** (Stanford U) **Lessons to be learned about discipline from alternative high schools.** *Journal of Research & Development in Education,* 1978(Sum), Vol 11(4), 78-91. —Disciplinary problems in alternative schools are fewer and less severe than in conventional schools. Suggestions are made as to how conventional schools can reduce problem behavior. (38 ref) —*T. Hodapp.*

    a. 2058 _____

    b. Perry, Cheryl L. and Duke, Daniel L._____

    c. Lessons to be learned about discipline from alternative high schools
    _____

d. *Journal of Research and Development in Education*

_____

e. 1978 (Sum) _____   h. 78- 91 _____

f. 11 _____   i. T. Hodapp _____

g. (4) _____

26. Fill in the term that correctly completes each statement.

   a. A summary of a periodical article is called a(n)_____.

   b. _____ is the list of indexing services in the Reference Area arranged by subject and by title.

   c. A(n) _____ includes all the information needed to find the article in a periodical.

   d. A(n) _____ arranged indexing service is one which requires the use of a separate **Subject Index**.

   e. The Library term used for magazine, periodical, or journal is _____.

   f. A(n) _____ gives citations to periodical articles.

   g. A(n) _____ arranged indexing services is one which has references following the subject.

Serials Catalog

Circle the correct answer for Questions 27 and 28.

27. The *ISU Serials Catalog-Titles* lists:

   a. All serials published
   b. All serials available in the ISU Library's Collection.
   c. Only the serials currently being received at ISU
   d. All serials available at the ISU Library except newspapers

28.   A copy of the *ISU Serials Catalog* is located:

   a. On each floor and tier of the Library
   b. At each service desk
   c. In each of the reading rooms around campus
   d. All of the above

Refer to these entries from the *ISU Serials Catalog* to answer the questions following each entry.

29.
```
JOURNAL OF POLITICAL ECONOMY
    V.1- ; DEC. 1892-
        HB1 .J83
        MICRO; 1-; 1892-; MICROFILM EDITION
        GEN; 1-61, 63-; 1892-; EXCEPT CURRENT ISSUES
        PER;    CURRENT ISSUES
        ECON; 53-; 1945-
```

   a. What is the call number? _____ _____

   b. What is the date of the first issue published?_____

   c. Volume 1 is located in what two places?_____ _____

   d. Volume 62 is located in what two places? _____ _____

   e. The latest issue is located in what two places? _____ _____

   f. The 1946 issues are located in what three places?
   _____
   _____
   _____

   g. What is the first (oldest) volume available in the Economics Reading Room?
   _____

30.
```
THE JOURNAL OF BUSINESS STRATEGY.
    VOL. 1, NO. 1 (SUMMER 1980)-
        HD28 .J593
        GEN; (2), 3-; 1982-; EXCEPT CURRENT ISSUES
        PER:    CURRENT ISSUES
```

   a. What is the call number? _____ _____

   b. What do the parentheses [( )] around "2" mean?
   _____

c. Is Volume 1 available in the ISU Library?_____

d. The latest issue is located where? _____

e. Are the current issues bound or unbound?_____

Use an *ISU Serials Catalog* in the Reference Area to answer the following:

31. Find one of the following corporate bodies and find it in the *ISU Serials Catalog--Corporate Body Index.* (The blue section of Volume 2) Give the first publication listed under each organization.

    a. NATIONAL SCIENCE TEACHER ASSOCIATION

    _____

    b. NATIONAL WILDLIFE FEDERATION

    _____

    c. IOWA STATE HORTICULTURAL SOCIETY

    _____

Serials Catalog Arrangement

32. Circle the letter of the choice which makes each of the following statements correct.

    a. In the *ISU Serials Catalog, Journal of Industrial Relations* is found
    (A) before; (B) between; (C) after; the two titles given below.

    Journal of the Faculty of Science

    Journal of the History

    b. In the *ISU Serials Catalog, J.K. Lasser's Your Income Tax* is found
    (A) before; (B) between; (C) after; the two titles given above.

    c. In the *ISU Serials Catalog, Journal of the Astronomy Society* is found
    (A) before; (B) between; (C) after; the two titles given above.

    d. In the *ISU Serials Catalog, Journal and Letters of History* is found
    (A) before; (B) between; (C) after; the two titles given above.

33. Which library tool listed on the right would you use to start looking for the following items. Some may have two correct answers.

a._____ The *Journal of Marine Research*   1. Titles and Author Section--Card Catalog

b._____ A biography (book) about George Bush   2. SCHOLAR2

c._____ A book written by Willa Cather   3. Serials Catalog--Titles

d._____ A citation to a periodical article about employment 4. Serials Catalog--Corporate Body Index

e._____ A list of the serial publications from the National Center for Health Statistics   5. An appropriate indexing service

f._____ A book titled *Centennial*   6. Subject Section--Card Catalog

g._____ *U.S. News and World Report* magazine

h._____ A book about computer science
       Library of Congress Subject Headings

34. Use the *Library of Congress Subject Headings* found near the SCHOLAR2 terminal on first floor to answer the following questions.

    a. What term would you use to find books about **yard sales**? _____

    b. What is a broader term (**BT**) to use when looking for books about **rock music**? _____

    c. How many narrower terms (**NT**) are listed under the subject, **rock music**?_____

    d. What are the three related terms (**RT**) listed under the subject, **benevolence**?_____

102

Card Catalog and SCHOLAR2

35. Circle the kinds of materials that you can find in the Card Catalog.

    a. Newspapers   c. Audio-visual materials
    b. Books   d. Magazines

36. Answer the following questions about the sample Card Catalog card shown below.

```
                    SOLAR HEATING.
    TH7413
    A5      Anderson, Bruce, 1947-
    1977       Solar energy : fundamentals in
            building design / Bruce Anderson. --
            New York : McGraw-Hill, c1977.
               374 p. : ill. ; 25 cm.
            HOLDINGS:
    DESIGN

    GEN
            Bibliography: p. [359]-370.
            Includes index.




    IaAS    &r repl. set. 2-19-80 IWANsc   76-45467r79
```

a. What is the call number for this book?_____

b. What is the copyright date?_____

c. Who is the publisher?_____

d. How many numbered pages does this book have?_____

e. Where are copies of the book available?_____
_____

f. What is the title of this book?_____
_____

g. Is the book illustrated?_____

103

h. Does it have a bibliography?_____

i. Who is the author?_____

j. What kind of card is this? (Circle one)

    author   title   subject

SCHOLAR2 QUESTIONS

Use a SCHOLAR2 terminal to complete the following exercises.

Try this title search.

    t prison and the prisoner

37. Who is the author of this book? _____

38. What is the call number and location of this book? _____
_____

Try this author search.

    a jones howard

39. Look at the <u>guide screen</u>. How many entries are there? _____

40. Look at the <u>index screen</u>. Did a Howard Jones write any books about prisons? _____

Try this subject search.

    S imprisonment

41. How many records are there? _____

Try this keyword search using the truncation symbol $

    k jail$

Browse through some of the records. Look for the word jail, jailer, jails, etc. to see where the term is found in each record. Note that it may be in any part of the record.

Try this keyword search with the Boolean operator **or**

    k jail$ or prisons

Remember that **or** broadens your search to give you more records.

Try this keyword search with the Boolean operator **and**

    k prisons and legislation

Remember that **and** narrows your search to give you fewer records.

APPENDIX F

ANSWERS TO THE SELF-HELP QUESTIONS

ANSWERS TO LOCATIONS AND SERVICE QUESTIONS

1. a
2. b
3. f
4. c
5. d
6. a
7. h
8. e
9. i
10. g
11. j
12. b
13. a
14. c

ANSWERS TO LOCATING PUBLICATIONS QUESTIONS

15. a. floor 2
    b. floor 3
    c. floor 3
    d. lower level
    e. tier 1
    f. floor 4

ANSWERS TO CIRCULATION PRINT-OUT QUESTIONS

16. a. No
    b. 5-13
    c. Reserve
    d. No Leisure Reading Room
    e. Recall it.

ANSWERS TO CALL NUMBER QUESTIONS

17. a. 1 c. 2
    b. 2 d. 2

18. a. 3 d. 1
    b. 3 e. 3
    c. 5 f. 1

19. a. 1 c. 2
    b. 3 d. 3

ANSWERS TO INDEXING SERVICES QUESTIONS

20. Any two of these five:
    Design Abstracts International
    Graphic Arts Abstracts
    Graphic Arts
    Literature Abstracts
    The Design Index

21. a. table 8
    b. A/I AT101 S24

22. a. alphabetically
    b. subject heading
    c. activities; Great Britain
    d. a citation
    e. 1. Challenge a child at play: a learning experience
       2. A. B. Etkes
       3. *Am Sch Bd J*
       4. 153
       5. 26-28
       6. August 1966
       7. yes

23. c.

24. a. Advertising Deception
    b. Graduate School of Business Administration, the University of Michigan
    c. R. J. Harris, et al.
    d. Training consumer about misleading advertising, transfer of training and effects of specialized knowledge.
    e. J. H. Leigh and C. R. Martin, Jr.
    f. *Current Issues in Research and Advertising*
    g. 1981
    h. 105-122
    i. Two experiments were performed to train subjects not to interpret or

25. a. reference number
    b. authors of title
    c. title of article
    d. title of journal
    e. date
    f. volume   g. issue
    h. pages   i. author of abstract

26. a. abstract
    b. *Guide to Indexing Services*
    c. citation
    d. numerical
    e. serial
    f. indexing service
    g. alphabetically

ANSWERS TO ISU SERIALS CATALOG QUESTIONS

27. b

28. d

29. a. HB1 J83
    b. December 1892
    c. Microforms; General Collection
    d. Microforms Center; Economics/Sociology Reading Room
    e. Periodical Room; Economics/Sociology Reading Room
    f. Microforms Center; General Collection; Economic/Sociology Reading Room
    g. volume 53

30. a. HD28 J593
    b. Some issues of that volume are missing
    c. No
    d. Periodical Room
    e. unbound

31. a. *Science and Children*
    b. *Conservation News*
    c. *Forestry Annual*
    d. *American Journal of Botany*

32. a. c   c. c
    b. a   d. a

33. a. 3   e. 4
    b. 2 or 6   f. 1 or 2
    c. 2 or 1   g. 2 or 3
    d. 5   h. 2 or 6

ANSWERS TO LIBRARY OF CONGRESS SUBJECT HEADINGS

34. a. garage sales
    b. popular music
    c. 8
    d. charity, humanity, kindness

35. b and c

36. a. TH7413 A5 1977
    b. 1977
    c. McGraw- Hill
    d. 374
    e. Design and General Collection
    f. Solar energy, fundamentals in building design
    g. yes
    h. yes
    i. Bruce Anderson
    j. subject

ANSWERS TO SCHOLAR2 QUESTIONS

37. Dorothy Tompkins
38. HV 8665 A11 T6
39. 43 or more
40. yes
41. 31 or more

Glossary

Abstract	A brief summary of the principal ideas of a book or periodical article.
Almanac	A collection of frequently needed facts and statistics gathered from many sources and reprinted in one volume.
Atlas	A collection of maps in book form.
Bibliographic Instruction	Instruction in the strategies used for locating information and conducting research.
Biography	A written account of a person's life.
Books, parts of	In order of their appearance.

    Title page--a page at the beginning of a volume that indicates the author, title and publication information.

    Preface or foreword--a preliminary note stating the purpose of the book, acknowledging the help of others.

    Table of contents--a list of the chapters of a book in the order in which they appear with an indication of the page on which they begin.

    Introduction--a description of the scope and level of the text material; it may also describe the manner of organization.

    Text--the main part of the book.

    Glossary--a list explaining the uncommon words not explained in the text.

    Appendix--supplementary material important to have in conjunction with the text.

    Bibliography--a list of source materials or references used in preparation of the text.

    Index--a detailed alphabetical list of topics, names, and places mentioned in the text.

Boolean logic	Use of the connectors **and, or,** and **not** to combine concepts involved in research and in conjunction with computerized literature searching.
Call number	A combination of letters and numbers assigned to a book or periodical in the library's collection to differentiate it from all others so that it can be arranged on the shelf.
Catalog	A tool used to learn what a library owns and where it is located; it is created using a uniform set of principles to describe materials in a collection.
CD-ROM	Compact Disk--Read Only Memory; optical information storage on a disk which allows a high amount of data such as references from a periodical index to be stored in a small space.
Citation	A reference supplying all information needed to identify and locate a given information source such as author, title, volume number, or publisher.
Classification	System used by libraries to arrange materials according to their subjects; the Iowa State University Library uses the Library of Congress Classification System.
Copyright	Legal provision granting an author, artist, or composer, an exclusive right to reproduce or distribute a work. This right may be transferred to a publisher or others.
Corporate author	A group responsible for the intellectual content of a work, such as an organization or corporation.
Cross reference	A direction from one heading or entry to another.
Database	An organized collection of computer records in a standardized format that can be stored and accessed in a variety of computer modes.

Depository	A library designated to receive all or some of the publications of a group such as the U.S. or state government and make them available to the public.
Dictionary	A source of information about words, including their meaning, pronunciation, spelling, derivation, and usage.
Directory	An alphabetical or classified list containing the names and addresses and often phone numbers of the inhabitants or organizations connected with a particular profession or occupation such as the American Psychiatric Association; also telephone directories.
Encyclopedia	A book or set of books that provide introductory or background information on all branches of knowledge or on specific areas of a special subject.
Entry	The record of an item in a catalog or an index. Also, in library cataloging, the specific points of access for locating information, including author, title, and subject.
Fair use	Conditions that permit copying for purposes such as teaching, scholarship, amd research where it is not necessary to obtain special permission from the copyright holder.
Floor	Designation for one of the four levels of the new additions to the Library used to house publications.
General Collection	The total of the floors and tiers; those areas in the Parks Library used to house the major portion of the Library's collection.
Handbook	Ready reference sources for given fields of knowledge used for quick location of facts related to the field.
Holdings	The volumes and/or issues of a publication that the Library owns.

Index	An alphabetical listing of the contents of a book, journal, or collection. Also a periodical index, which classifies the contents of journals providing subject access.
Interlibrary loan	A procedure for borrowing from another library those materials not available in this library.
Journal	A periodical containing scholarly articles.
Magazine	A periodical containing general interest articles.
Main entry	In a catalog or an index, the entry under which the most complete bibliographic information is given.

Microform	A reproduction in a size too small to be read by the unaided eye.
	    Microfiche--transparent 4" x 6" sheet of film
	    Microfilm--usually 35 mm

Monograph	A work, collection, or other writing that is not a serial; usually a book.
Online terminal	A terminal directly connected to the central processing unit of a computer system.
Periodical	A magazine or other serial publication for which issues appear at regular or stated intervals.
Plagiarism	The use of materials without crediting the source; presenting as an original idea, interpretation, or organization derived from an existing source.
Serial	A publication planned to be published on a continuing basis (newspaper, journal, magazine).

Series	A group of separate items related to one another by the fact that each item in the group bears a collective title applying to the whole group.
Subject headings	A word or group of words under which all materials dealing with a given subject are entered in an index, catalog, or bibliography.
Thesaurus	A dictionary of synonyms; in research, often a list of standardized subject headings, with cross references from nonused terms to those used in a particular indexing system or database.
Tier	Designation for one of the seven levels in the original part of the building housing part of the General Collection.
Truncation	The process of using a shortened form of a word to look for all forms of the word, as in a computer database.

Name _____ Section ____ Instructor _____

SEARCH STRATEGY ASSIGNMENT

Purpose: Completing this assignment will help you understand the research process you will use when gathering information for papers and projects required in other classes.

The assignment requires you to complete the following components of the research process. Directions for completing each section are given later.

A. Choose one subject from a given list of topics and narrow its focus.
B. Formulate a search strategy for finding information on this topic, by identifying:
    1. A subject encyclopedia which might provide general background information on the topic.
    2. A book which might provide more specific information on the topic. You will use SCHOLAR2 to do this.
    3. A periodical article which relates to the topic. You will use either a print or CD-ROM index to do this.
C. Evaluate the periodical article.

NOTE: "Academic dishonesty occurs when a student submits as his or her own work products prepared by another person. Such behavior is abhorrent to the university." (*ISU Information Handbook*)

YOU ARE EXPECTED TO TURN IN A UNIQUE ASSIGNMENT.

CHOOSING AND NARROWING A TOPIC

ASSIGNMENT TOPICS

Home Schooling	Collegiate Athletics
Famine	Cable Television
Advertising	Recycling
Nuclear Power	Computer Aided Design (CAD)
Volcanoes	Earthquakes
Ethics	Censorship
Grant Wood	Impressionism

1.   What general topic did you select from the list above?_____

2.   To what general area of study will you relate the topic you selected? (i.e. art, business, science, social science, education, etc.) _____

Narrow this topic.

3. In one sentence describe a narrower aspect of this topic on which you might focus a 5-page paper?

_____

_____

FINDING BACKGROUND INFORMATION

From the following list of subject encyclopedias, circle the letter of the one that would most likely have an overview of the topic you selected.
   a. *Encyclopedia of Bioethics*
   b. *Encyclopedia of Religion and Ethics*
   c. *Encyclopedia of Economics*
   d. *McGraw-Hill Encyclopedia of Science and Technology*
   e. *Encyclopedia of Crime and Justice*
   f. *Encyclopedia of Social Work*
   g. *Encyclopedia of the American Judicial System*
   h. *World Encyclopedia of Political Systems and Parties*
   i. *Encyclopedia of Social Sciences*
   j. *Handbook of American Popular Culture*
   k. *Encyclopedia of Educational Research*
   l. *Harvard Encyclopedia of American Ethnic Groups*

Use SCHOLAR2 to determine the call number and location for the title you selected from the above list.

4. What is the call number and location for the title you selected?

_____

FINDING DETAILED INFORMATION: BOOKS

Use *Library of Congress Subject Headings* found near the SCHOLAR2 terminals on the first floor to find the correct term to search for your topic.

5. What term would you use? (List only one, even if more than one is given).

_____

Use SCHOLAR2 and the *Library of Congress Subject Heading* you have identified to do a subject search and find one book title on your topic. Use a terminal with a printer. **Print the screen which answers questions 6 and 7. ATTACH TO THIS ASSIGNMENT.**

6. What is the book's title?_____

_____

7. What is the book's call number? _____

8. On what floor or tier would it be shelved? _____ Floor or _____ Tier

FINDING DETAILED INFORMATION: PERIODICALS

Use a subject index to magazines and journals. Choose from the list of indexes below the one most likely to provide information on your topic. Circle the letter of the index you will use.

    a. *Social Sciences Index* (CD-ROM format)
    b. *Social Sciences Index* (print) Table 1
    c. *Applied Science and Technology Index* (CD-ROM format)
    d. *Applied Science and Technology Index* (print) Table 9
    e. *Business Periodicals Index* (CD-ROM format)
    f. *Business Periodicals Index* (print) Table 4
    g. *Education Index* (print only) Table 6
    h. *General Science Index* (print only) Table 5
    i. *Humanities Index* (print only) Table 2
    j. *Art Index* (print only) Table 6
    k. *Biological and Agricultural Index* (print only) Table 8

Find this index title in the Reference Room.

9. If you used a print index, which volume of the index did you use? _____

10. Whether you used a print index or one on CD-ROM, under what subject term did you find relevant material for your topic? _____

11. Choose a citation to one article on the subject listed in question 10. If you are using a print index, copy the citation exactly as it appears in the index. If you are using a CD-ROM index print the screen which has the citation you want and attach it to this assignment.
_____
_____

In the print index, on what page was the citation? _____

Use the citation in number 11 or on your CD-ROM print-out to answer number 12.

12.   a. Author (if given) _____
      b. Title of the article _____
_____

      c. Complete unabbreviated title of periodical in which article appears
_____

      d. Volume and/or Issue Number(s)_____
      e. Pages _____ f. Date _____

REMEMBER TO ATTACH A COPY OF THE SCREEN WHICH HAS YOUR CITATION IF YOU USED A CD-ROM INDEX.

SEARCHING FOR THE PERIODICAL

The *ISU Serials Catalog* and SCHOLAR2 contain the same information about the Library's periodical holdings. Either can be used to determine if the Library owns a particular title. At this time it is easier to use the *ISU Serials Catalog*. Look for the periodical title listed in 12-c in the *ISU Serials Catalog*.

13. Did you find the title? _____ Yes _____ No

If you did not find the title you will not be able to do the rest of this assignment. This is o.k.

14. If "yes," what is the call number? _____

15. Check all locations where you could find this periodical title for the date listed in 12-f.

    _____ General Collection, give floor_____ or tier _____
    _____ Periodical Room
    _____ Microforms Center
    _____ Design Reading Room
    _____ Economics/Sociology Reading Room
    _____ Physical Sciences Reading Room
    _____ Veterinary Medicine Library
    _____ Mathematics Reading Room

If the article you are looking for is in one of the first three locations listed above, photocopy the first page of your article and attach it to the assignment. If you do not find the issue which has your article, and it should be in the General Collection give the stack range where it should be and the color of the bound volumes of that title.

EVALUATING THE ARTICLE

Read through the article or skim if lengthy.

16. Was the article relevant to the topic?

    _____ Yes _____ No

17. Which best describes the article?

    _____ Research _____ Popular

18. Did the article have a bibliography?
    _____ Yes _____ No

INDEX

A
Abstracting services, 50
Abstracts, 50, 51
Access to information, history of, 11
Administrative Offices, 24
Almanacs, 13
Alphabetical indexes, 49
APA Guide, 82
Archives, 25
Atlases, 23
Audio cassette tour, 21
Author search, 63

B
Bibliographic Instruction Department Office, 18
Books, 33
Boolean logic, 54, 56, 67
Brainstorming, 29, 30
Broader term (BT), 65

C
Call number, definition, 4
Call number, order, 38, 39, 40, 41
Card Catalog, 4, 17, 71
Catalog, 4, 13
Cataloging, 4
CBE Style Manual, 82
CD-ROM, Compact disk--Read Only Memory, 47, 5
Checklist, research techniques, 34
Chicago Manual of Style, 83
Circulation Desk, 17
Citation Numbers, 50
Citations, 44, 45, 46
Classification Systems, 11
Classifying, 4
Computerized Literature Searching, 54
Connectors, 56, 66
Conservation and preservation rules, 5
Context Broadening, 31
Controlled Vocabulary Thesaurus, 13

119

Copyright laws, 7
County City Data Book, 57
Crossreferences, 49

D
Database, 54
Dewey Decimal System, 11
Dictionaries, 13
Dictionary of Military Terms, 13
Direction Kiosk
Directory, 13

E
Elevators, Location, 17
Encyclopedias, 13, 17

F
Filing rules, 72, 73
Focus, narrowing 30
Full text databases, 11

G
General Collection, 22
General Index, 12
Geological maps, 22
Government Publications, 17, 22
Grant Wood Foyer, 18
Grolier Electronic Encyclopedia, 57
Group study rooms, 24
Guide to Indexing Services, 47, 48, 51, 57

I
Indexing services, use of, 44
Information, 3
Information Desk, 17
Information, evaluating, 33
Interlibrary Loan procedures, 18
Interlibrary Loan Office, 18
Iowa State University Information Handbook, 6
ISU Serials Catalog, 74-78

J
Journals, 32, 44

K
Keyword searching, 66, 67
Knowledge, 3

L
Library card, 17
Library of Congress Classification System, 11, 38
Library of Congress Subject Headings, 65

M
Magazines, 32, 44
Map Room, 23
Media Center, 21
Microfiche, 18
Microfilm, 18
Microform format, 18, 48
Microforms Center, 18
Microprint, 18
MLA Handbook, 83

N
Narrow term (NT), 65
New Book Room, 18
Newspapers, 31, 46
Numerical (two-step) indexes, 50

O
Official Congressional Directory, 13
Online Public Access Catalog, 4, 60
Overdue fines, 17

P
Parks, William Robert and Ellen Sorge, 17
People, as sources, 33
Periodical indexes, 11
Periodical Room, 23
Periodical, definition, 44
Photoduplication Office, 17
Plagiarism, 6
Portable microfiche reader, 18
Primary research, 6

R
Rare books, 25
Reference sources, 13
Reference Area, 17
Reference Collection, 17
Reference Desk, 17
Related term (RT), 65
Research, topic, 28, 39
Reserve Reading Room, 18
Reserve Desk, 18
Restrooms, location, 17
Roget's Thesaurus, 13

S
SCHOALR2, 17, 60-70
SCHOLAR2 screens, 61, 61, 63, 64, 68, 69, 70
Scholarship, 3
Search terms, 30
Search strategy, 28, 34, 35
SEARCHLINE, 47, 54, 57
Secondary research, 6
Secondary sources, 12
See also, (SA) 49
Seminar Room, 18
Serials, 44
Serials Catalog, (steps to use), 74-78
Serials Information Window, 23
Sources, uses, 31-33
Special Collections, 25
Stacks, 23
Subject Headings, 65
Subject index, 50
Subject search, 64
Subject specific index, 13
Synonyms, (in searches) 30

T
Technical Services Area, 23
Tertiary sources, 12
Theft, (of personal belongings) 23
Thesaurus, 13
Title search, 62, 68
Topographic maps, 22
Traditional thesaurus, 13
Turabian, Kate, 83

U-Z
Used for, (UF) 65
Webster's New Collegiate Dictionary, 13
Welcome screen, 61
Who's Who, 13
World Book Encyclopedia, 13
WPA Artists, 18
Yearbooks, 17